THE MAKING OF BARBARIANS

translation
TRANSNATION

SERIES EDITOR **EMILY APTER**

A list of titles in the series appears at the back of the book.

The Making of Barbarians

CHINESE LITERATURE AND MULTILINGUAL ASIA

HAUN SAUSSY

PRINCETON UNIVERSITY PRESS

PRINCETON & OXFORD

Published by Princeton University Press
41 William Street, Princeton, New Jersey 08540
99 Banbury Road, Oxford OX2 6JX

press.princeton.edu

All Rights Reserved

First paperback printing, 2024
Paper ISBN 9780691231983
Cloth ISBN 9780691231976
ISBN (e-book) 9780691231969

Library of Congress Control Number: 2021949467

British Library Cataloging-in-Publication Data is available

Editorial: Anne Savarese, James Collier
Jacket/Cover Design: Karl Spurzem
Production: Erin Suydam
Publicity: Alyssa Sanford, Charlotte Coyne
Copyeditor: Anita O'Brien

Jacket/Cover art: *Eighteen Songs of a Nomad Flute: The Story of Lady Wenji*, unidentified artist, early 15th century, Ming Dynasty (1368–1644). Ex coll.: C.C. Wang Family, Gift of the Dillon Fund, 1973.

This book is published with the generous support of Research Center for Chinese Cultural Subjectivity in Taiwan at National Chengchi University

This book has been composed in Arno

Es ist niemals ein Dokument der Kultur, ohne zugleich ein solches der Barbarei zu sein.

(There is no document of civilization which is not at the same time a document of barbarism.)

—WALTER BENJAMIN, "THESES ON THE
PHILOSOPHY OF HISTORY"

the earth the sky the people around him the fruit the shops, it was all one and the same, all of it and him, and this kind of a feeling he always gave to them who saw him walking standing thinking talking, that the world was all him, there was no difference in it in him, and the fruit inside or outside him there were no separations of him or from him, and the whole world he lived in always lived inside him.

—GERTRUDE STEIN, THE MAKING OF AMERICANS

To the memory of Paul Edward Farmer (1959–2022)
Tout moun sé moun

CONTENTS

Introduction

Intrinsically Extrinsic

物无非彼，物无非是

AS WE LEARN in our first encounters with the Chinese language
and civilization (for some, this event takes place practically at
birth), the adjective that qualifies China in Chinese is *Zhong* 中,
"center" or "inward"; what is not Chinese is *wai* 外, "outside."[1] "In"
and "out" are what we call in English prepositions: they describe
relations, not essences. Over the long course of Chinese civilization, some practices or values have often been singled out as the
core or essence of Chineseness: the *zhong* of the *Zhong*, as it were.
My many years of fascination with China have not led me in that
direction. The inquiry conducted in this book goes relationally
and indirectly, asking how the *wai* defines the *zhong* for one of
those practices deemed to be closest to the civilization's core: writing, the effort to shape the world through and as a system of enduring traces. In other words, it is about the outside seen from the
inside, as reconstructed by an outsider.

My inquiry into the intrinsic, the extrinsic, and the literary
has taken shape in the space between two quotations from the
early Chinese empire. First we have the proud proclamation of
sovereign centrality and commonality, achieved through the

First Emperor's unification of *Tianxia* (All under Heaven) in 221 BCE:

今天下車同軌，書同文，行同倫。

Now, throughout the world, cart-tracks are of one width; writing is with the same characters; and for conduct there are the same rules.[2]

And next we have the no less proud prediction, deduced from Zhang Qian's 張騫 report of 125 BCE to Emperor Wu of the Han 漢武帝, that news of the Chinese sovereign's glory would attract people as yet unaware of any such unification of cartwheels, morals, and written marks:

天子既聞大宛及大夏、安息之屬皆大國，多奇物，土著，頗與中國同業，而兵弱，貴漢財物；其北有大月氏、康居之屬，兵彊，可以略遺設利朝也。且誠得而以義屬之，則廣地萬里，重九譯，致殊俗，威德遍於四海。[3]

Thus the emperor learned of Dayuan [Ferghana], Daxia [Bactria], Anxi [Parthia], and the rest, all great states rich in unusual products whose people cultivated the land and made their living in much the same way as the Chinese. All these states, he was told, were militarily weak and prized Han goods and wealth. He also learned that to the north of them lived the Yuezhi [Tocharian] and Kangju [Sogdian] people who were strong in arms but could be persuaded by gifts and the prospect of gain to acknowledge allegiance to the Han court. If it were only possible to win over these states by peaceful means, the emperor thought, he could then extend his domain [by] 10,000 *li*, attract to his court men of strange customs and languages requiring ninefold translation, and his might would become known to all the lands within the four seas.[4]

"Nine" is here a rhetorically vivid substitute for "many." The hypothetical "ninefold translation," *jiu yi* 九譯 as it is usually abbreviated, is a bucket-brigade scenario of international communication, the Chinese representative speaking to a bilingual Sogdian, who speaks to a bilingual Bactrian, who speaks to a bilingual Parthian, and so on. Such chains of translation would both spread the news of China and add to its majesty by linking to the centers of other worlds inhabited by people as yet undiscovered.

Within China, a unified script; outside it, the need for nine (or infinite) levels of translating. Between these poles arise complementary profiles of Self and Other, or Similar and Different, which I have sought to investigate through textual records. To those who know it, of course, China is not all the same. The cart tracks, even if cut to a standard width, wind through thousands of mountains and valleys and plains, each area unlike all the others. The words are pronounced in hundreds of different ways from place to place. The people go by one or another of the Hundred Surnames: the Zhangs, the Lis, the Chens, the Wangs. . . . But all these differences are linked, regulated, relativized by shared communicative norms. If the great achievement of the unified Chinese empire, according to the first quotation, is the imposition of a single set of rules, foreign cultures, as in the second quotation, are a proliferation of endless unregulated and unpredictable differences. The contrast is stark and so often repeated that its details are easily lost to consciousness. If in China everything is Similar, and if outside of it Difference reigns, the differences are not apt to matter very much to a person inside the circle of Similarity. If the meaning of the contrast of Similarity and Difference is its pertinence to saying something about the realm of the Similar, then it cannot matter very much what local differences arise in the land of the Different, or (to get a bit more specific) what the languages and peoples of the ninefold translation relays are. "They" are perceivable as "not-us"; "we" are tautologically "ourselves." But if we consider the unity and diversity signaled by these quotations not as static facts but as processes, then the contrast takes on a different sense. It is not just that Chinese are one way and outsiders are another; how they got to be that way is the question. In that perspective, Chinese homogeneity results from a conquest (never quite complete) of matter by sovereign will, and foreign diversity becomes tangible through the coordination of incomprehensible tongues, an "organization of distances" aimed at creating intelligibility for the Chinese end-listener.[5] Who exactly are these foreigners whose desire to enter into communication with China, or whose products' attractiveness to the Chinese, magnetizes their outlandish idioms into a noisy chorus ending at the palace gate? It would be a pity to fold those nine acts of translation into a single concept, even an encompassing one such as foreignness, diversity, or plurality.

The chapters of this book ask in different ways about the specifics of those nine relays, those strange customs, and about what happens once they come into contact with Sinographic culture. While being a devoted reader of Chinese, that is, central, texts, I practice the eccentric discipline of comparative literature.[6] Centrality and eccentricity meet here in a loopy dance, a parabolic orbit.

———

Comparative literature? But isn't that an essentially Eurocentric discipline? Even when it tries to be accommodating, comparative literature expresses its origins. Goethe in 1827 had an intuition that "national literature means little now, and the era of world literature is at hand"; he was brought to that revelation by reading a translated Chinese novel.[7] Marx and Engels declared in the *Communist Manifesto* (1848) that "the bourgeoisie has through its exploitation of the world market given a cosmopolitan character to production and consumption in every country," so that "from the numerous national and local literatures, there arises a world literature."[8] In this understanding, which is by now widespread, the "world" of "world literature" is a side effect of the "world system," latterly known as globalization, understood as a network of political and economic relations set in motion by Columbus's voyages and the subsequent implantation of European colonies on all the continents.[9] And indeed accounts of the progress of world or comparative literature are usually written around a European center and protagonist. For example, the editorial of the first number (1903) of Columbia University's *Journal of Comparative Literature* claimed for comparatists a "new citizenship in the rising state which—the obscurer or brighter dream of all great scholars from Plato to Goethe—is without frontiers or race or force, but there reason is supreme."[10] The "unity of mankind" and "upbuilding of the international state in a homogeneous civilization" to which George Woodberry, the journal's editor, looked forward were to be achieved by comparative scholarship capable of identifying the universals in literature and culture. After a solid basis had been achieved in European languages, Woodberry foresaw "the approaching exploitation of the old literatures of the Orient, which is the next great event in the literary history of the world." But those "old literatures" long preexisted Goethe and, for some of them, Plato too; only those literatures' unfamiliarity in the eyes of European latecomers made their "exploitation" "the next great event" in literary history. What would happen if our histories of literature began from those centers and progressed through the ages toward the discovery of those Europeans still living, at a recent date, "in the forests," as Goethe delicately put it?

———

The term "comparative literature" in China is a little over a hundred years old. The act of comparison that began it is indeed a meeting of the *Zhong* 中 and the *wai* 外 on the premises of the *Zhong*.

文學進化觀念的第二層意義是：每一類文學不是三年兩載就可以發達完備的，須是從極低微的起原，慢慢的，漸漸的，進化到完全發達的地位。有時候，這種進化剛到半路上，遇着阻力，就停住不進步了...

一種文學有時進化到一個地位，便停住不進步了；直到他與別種文學相接觸，有了比較，無形之中受了影響，或是有

意的吸收人的長處，方才再繼續有進步．．． 我現在且不說這
種「比較的文學研究」可以得到的種種高深的方法與觀念。[11]

The concept of literary evolution has two layers of meaning: no literature flourishes and comes to fruition overnight, it must rather arise from small beginnings and slowly, step by step, progress to a state of complete development. Sometimes this process of evolution is blocked in midcourse, stops, and then there is no more progress. . . .

A literature sometimes evolves to a certain stage, comes to a stop and makes no more progress. It is only through contact with other literatures that it is able to make comparisons, and either be influenced unconsciously or deliberately incorporate the strengths of others: then and only then progress may continue. . . . For the moment I will not go into the many great and deep methods and concepts that are to be derived from such "comparative literary research."

As an assertion of a bare kind of causality in the cultural realm, Hu Shi's statement can hardly be faulted: sometimes a literary tradition runs out of things to say, repeats itself, becomes sterile or loses relevance, and awaits new impetus from outside. But the abstract language hides a more specific referent. Hu Shi in 1918 was not talking about enacting comparisons with just any "other": the other relevant at the time to comparison with Chinese literature was "the West," meaning chiefly modern literature in English, French, Russian, German, and Japanese. East-West comparison, of which this is by no means the first instance, had already risen to the status of obsession in philosophies of history and theories of national identity in both Europe and Asia, but Hu Shi here initiates the phrase *bijiao [de] wenxue* 比較 [的] 文學 and molds the practices that would come to define it. Such East-West comparison served a specific purpose.[12] The aim was not to come to know the countless variety of literary traditions around the world, including those of Asia, but to learn how to modernize ("develop") Chinese literature. And that is how discussions of *Zhongwai wenxue* 中外文學 (not the distinguished literary monthly, but the subject area, "Chinese-foreign literature") have grown up: a particular set of examples dominates very nearly to the point of defining it. The *wai* of *Zhongwai* refers, in common usage, to contemporary Europe and North America as the sites of present-day literary prestige.[13] Theirs are the literary artifacts with which it is interesting or valuable to compare China's. Any current comparative-literature journal's table of contents will bear this out: the *waiguo wenxue* 外國文學 (foreign literature) with which *Zhongguo wenxue* 中國文學 (Chinese literature) of any period and genre is associated is a selective, often hyperselective canon: Homer, Dante, Shakespeare, Baudelaire, Kafka, Joyce, Woolf. . . . The intelligent young people who come to me to write papers and dissertations often have in mind models of scholarship that follow these precedents. But why should those examples occupy the near-totality of the comparative space? They represent, at the very least, a narrow selection among the possible values for *wai*. What makes those the right examples for comparison? Why not other examples, of which there is no shortage? Scholars turn out comparative studies of Sima Qian and Herodotus (but not the *Nuremberg Chronicle*, Garcilaso de la Vega, or the Kirghiz epic of Manas); Li Bai and Keats (and not Jayadeva or Peire Vidal); or Cao Xueqin and Marcel Proust (and not Ann Radcliffe or Abdelkébir Khatifi)—I make no promises as to the fertility of these alternative suggestions, though something can be learned from any comparison; the question is why some comparisons are always made and others are seemingly never made.[14]

In poetics, the domain that habitually is my main concern, the practice of *zhongwai* research has long meant calling up a few examples from the traditions to be honored (Wordsworth and Wang Wei, Aristotle and Liu Xie, and so forth) and deriving from them principles said to characterize the Chinese literary universe. Polarities available for use in other areas of critical discourse serve to mark off what is specifically Chinese from what is "Western": metonymy versus metaphor, reality versus fiction, space versus time, nature versus consciousness, emulation versus originality, process versus product, index versus sign. The supposed impossibility of translation (I am not denying its difficulty) prompts talk of incommensurate cultural worlds or, what is almost the same, leads to frowning on translation as necessarily denaturing the pristine original.[15] There is an inescapable irony in the way this often defensively inaccessible Self has emerged from its (mis)representation by the Other. But the first step was choosing the Other by which to mediate the Self.

I am not calling for objectivity in this matter, only for a recognition of whatever it is that determines our selectivity. To speak of myself, I can hardly spend a waking hour without thinking of French literature in one way or another. But France is only one of the countries on the face of the earth, and I can't even claim it as my own; the imbalance of attention is not a pathology, just a consequence of my personal history, taste, intellectual loyalties, admirations, challenges, and so forth. The case of *Zhongwai*, involving such a mismatch between an inclusive term and its limited applications, similarly testifies to contemporary attitudes about the kinds of literature that deserve attention, the works and styles and movements with which it is desirable to compare Chinese works, the sorts of jobs that are available, and the sorts of claim about literature in general that our contemporaries like to make. The result, however, is presentism and self-reinforcing narrowness of scope. Just as with ocular vision and attention, focus on one object causes other objects to retreat from view.[16] The dominance of leading examples leads, a hundred years after Hu Shi's opening gesture, to repetition and sterility in a field.

"Might it be possible," Eric Hayot asks, "that another world-view, no longer dominated by the kinds of modern historiography that have given us the two-worlds model, could provoke new strategies of comparison?"[17] The heritage of *Zhongwai bijiao wenxue* 中外比較文學 as constructed under the "two-worlds model" seems to me to constitute a problem, however grateful I am for the insights and connections it has made possible.

Now that the imbalance inherent to *Zhongwai* cultural study has been brought into view, some might detect "privilege," some might adduce colonialism and self-colonization, some might point to practical constraints on language learning or commitment to national tasks; some might take the opportunity to call for a truly Chinese theory of *Zhongwai* cultural relations; but the response to the problem cannot lie in a reiteration of the polar scheme of Self and Other. Let us take a more inclusive inventory. There is a Self, partly consisting of internalized Others; there are Others; there are Other Others; there are Others who are so Other that they are not even recognized as Others; and a complex tissue of relationships binds them all. That fabric of relation is what we have an opportunity to rediscover in doing multilateral, comparative literary history.[18] In this book I am attempting to use the evidence of literary history—itself obviously biased in many ways—to restore some neglected objects to view, indeed to bring these usually silenced dialogue-partners into the conversation with the past that is literary history. To be specific, I will investigate the meanings that translation, adaptation, appropriation, and comparison of texts acquired on the boundaries of China long before Scottish merchants, Indian opium, and the British Navy began to interest the Qing court in the customs of Far Western peoples. The word *wai* has not always pointed to Europeans and Americans, nor has *xi* always designated an imaginary assemblage containing London, Paris, Berlin, New York, and California. I have stayed mostly within the boundaries of China and the Chinese language to pursue this first part of a larger investigation, attempting to show, first, how many different kinds of *wai* there are (enough to keep nine legions of translators busy, at least), and second, how many ways there are of relating to them, even if inveterate reflexes tend to press those relationships into a few set patterns. Looking beyond these chapters' scope and my own limited abilities, I am proposing that people interested in Chinese literature and the comparative viewpoint turn at least part of their attention away from the hypostatized West and toward China's historical neighbors, those with whom translation, even of the "ninefold" variety, was most necessary.

The investigation I offer to readers' attention here began with an invitation from the International Comparative Literature Association (ICLA) to begin planning a long-term, multiauthor project on the history of literary influences and developments in East Asia. Before that work could properly begin, I needed to take inventory of my own attitudes and knowledge. Motivating the ICLA's plan was the idea of overcoming the Eurocentrism of its previous research committees and practices. I see Eurocentrism as a failure in knowledge entailing moral shortcomings, akin to presentism. Not knowing, or not being curious to know, others outside our immediate realm of reference and value, we act as if they did not (or did not fully) exist, or as if they could exist only by being translated into languages and value schemes reducible to our own. One way to repair this flaw is by making available the missing knowledge. Although I claim no particular moral authority, my cognitive experience as someone who has been trying to learn Chinese for forty years may be pertinent. Starting from the provincial perspective of a place, a family, and a history, and slowly becoming acquainted with other places, families, and histories, often being scandalized or repelled by them, I managed to acquire some understanding of Europe, then of China, so that in my thoughts the reflexes of Eurocentrism could at least be questioned and tugged by those of Sinocentrism. But Sinocentrism too demands to be overcome, and for the same reasons. The self-concept of literarily educated Chinese depends on ideas about others and outsiders, and it is by asking about those ideas of the other that we can learn things about the shared self-conception that otherwise would never rise to consciousness. The way to bring these implications to the surface, as always, required attention to particular texts, terms, events, and patterns, rather than broad endorsements or dismissals. These chapters offer an account of how I learned to think about some others' others, which does not mean that the other of the other led back to the self—far from it.[19]

1

The Nine Relays:
Translation in China

殊方九譯之俗: 多語亞洲作為文學系統

THE TOPIC OF the five studies included in this volume is how cultural China has related to its outsides, before the modern period. The time limitation is important: before 1850 or so, writers in China never thought of themselves as being under a cultural or social deficit. They were at the center of their world, and the edges of that world were inhabited by less educated, less capable, less cultivated, less organized people—that was never in doubt. After the Opium Wars the situation began to change; I think this is uncontroversial. That moment forms the beginning of the modern period in China, as we understand it today. In the premodern period China is its own center; in the modern period Chinese begin to see themselves as inhabiting a margin, as needing to catch up with others, to adopt what are variously called modern, global, or Western standards of thinking, behavior, and expression.

Generally, when people narrate this shift in Chinese culture they are about to launch into an account of Chinese modernity, its various crises, exaltations, and tragedies. I am more interested in the pre-1850 situation because it offers more opportunities for thinking differently about the present, and that is something we definitely need, as the conventional categories for thinking about history, culture, and the world order begin to fail us. Such reference points as the First World, Second World, and Third World, or the "developed" and the "developing" worlds, or the free world and the socialist bloc, the Global North and Global South, the right and the left, the colonial powers and the anticolonial or decolonial forces, the elite and the mass, the neoliberal corporation and the social-democratic state no longer describe the situations we find ourselves in, although intoning such slogans brings the comfort of group conformity in the absence of analytic understanding. The stories we tell about China are, of course, threaded through all these categories and must, I think, be told anew in a longer historical perspective and with a greater readiness to face ambiguity. Admittedly, cultural geopolitics is a vast and unwieldy topic, suitable for prophets, ideologues, and visionaries, and I cannot claim to be one of those. As a way of finding legitimate access to that immensity, let us consider the narrower topic of translation.

Translation is a live subject everywhere in Asia today. But when we talk about translation in Asia, one type of example tends to dominate and occupy the whole subject: namely, translation between European languages and Chinese, Korean, and Japanese, as this has been practiced since about 1900. Translation includes, of course, communication in two directions: works getting translated from European languages into Asian languages, and works being translated from Asian languages into European ones. These are two vastly different types of translation, as we can see by just looking superficially at quantity and impact. In the China field, which is the only one I am competent to say anything about, the translation of foreign works arises simultaneously with the project of a modern literature, and so the study of translation tends to become identified with the study of this literature, which takes its models and effects from Russian, French, and English writing of the past two hundred years more conspicuously than from earlier Chinese poetry and fiction.[1] As Liang Qichao 梁啟超 wrote in 1920, "the second age of translation [in Chinese history] has arrived," alluding to the massive inflow of Buddhist translations between the

Han and Tang dynasties as the first age of translation.[2] And that second era of translation is not over. As Xie Shaobo puts it, translating modernity and translating China are more or less the same project; as Lydia Liu puts it, Chinese modernity is a translated modernity.[3]

The turn toward the foreign was not entirely voluntary. It was motivated by a feeling of lack, exhaustion, and defeat, as if the three-thousand-year history of China had finally run its course and needed to be replaced by something else. That rather extreme expression of marginality can stand for the profile that translation takes on when it is a channel of communication going in one direction, from center to periphery, from the "haves" (in terms of cultural value) to the "have-nots." A hundred years later, that dynamic is still active in our scholarly accounts, as those who recognize the importance of translation for modern Chinese literature and thought must also defend that recent tradition from the charges of derivativeness, marginality, and superficiality. So we see attention given—justly—to the aspects of selection, creative adaptation, and originality in the archive built up by Chinese translators since the late Qing.

On the other side of the communication channel, and taking the transmission in the opposite direction, the situation differs greatly. When texts from China are translated into French, English, or German, inter alia, the case is sometimes made that these are works that have the potential to transform the poetic language, the mental orientations, or the society and politics of the receiving cultures (for such affirmations, see the work of Ezra Pound, Joseph Needham, A. C. Graham, and Roger Ames, for example), but this belief is far from a majority one and is often taken as the mark of an unusual eccentricity. Moreover, in such acts of translation, the translator is highly visible (*pace* Lawrence Venuti's general argument that translation in the West enforces "invisibility" on the translator); we readily concede to Pound, Waley, or Hawkes the task of "inventing Chinese poetry for our time," and we may accept translations by people who do not actually know the language being translated from, because it is expected that the necessary information will be far out of the way of the ordinary reader and not subject to wider verification.[4] For inhabitants of a peripheral culture, translation is necessary, imposed, sometimes a lifeline; for inhabitants of a central culture, it is optional, decorative, at most educational. And quite apart from the individual personalities and motivations of the translators, we might add that translation into a dominant culture reinforces that cultural dominance. It adds a resource to the treasury of readers and thinkers who speak that major language; it expands their world and transfers a wealth of experience, making those already rich in prestige yet richer, rather than compensating for a perceived lack, as in the case of translation toward a less dominant language. Translation may be considered a means of public education. It does for readers at large what language learning does for individuals. It connects centers and margins at many scales. A bright kid who grows up speaking one of the minority languages of Russia or China will gain, by going to school and learning the national language, not only the cultural treasures of standard Russian or Mandarin, but all the things that have already been translated into those global languages. Learning a dominant language is not necessarily cultural surrender; it is generally useful.[5] Denouncing "the linguistic imperialism of neoliberal empire," as some have done in reference to global English, should not blind us to the real benefits conferred by acquiring a major world language.[6]

But situations change. English was not always a dominant language enjoying the "splendid isolation" that is its fate today: a fair number of our English classics, from Chaucer to Shakespeare to the King James Bible to the *Rubaiyyat*, the *Arabian Nights*, and the fairy tales of the Brothers Grimm, are translations. The ground may shift under a dominant language, or an unforeseen development may make a different language into a coveted resource for some or all speakers of the prestigious idiom. One such change is the abrupt shift in status of literary Chinese. Before about 1850, to be educated, for East Asian people, meant primarily to know literary Chinese. Those who had access to that archive of texts rarely gave much consideration to other literary traditions. There were bilingual, or more properly biliterate, cultures that used writing systems of their own, but Chinese was for them the language of higher prestige and wider circulation.[7] Starting in the 1860s, a wave of translations unseated Chinese from its dominant position—and these translations occurred not first in Chinese but in Japanese, with Russian being an important source language.[8] Thus we might observe an antagonism between literary Chinese and translation: when one is strong, the other is weak. In the longer perspective, given the cultural power of literary Chinese, translation is not a continuous practice in China; it is a discontinuous one; it becomes important at critical, exceptional moments and fades away otherwise; the usual mode of communication, over the three thousand years that I invite you to consider here, has been monolingual, within Chinese. In talking about translation in China, we will, therefore, be talking about exceptions to that general monolingual rule, and as always with exceptions, it's natural to ask why they emerge.

Every translation challenges ethnocentrism, at least implicitly. But not only that. A translation is always a negotiation. What will the market bear? What will the audience accept? How great is the appetite for things new and strange? Under the heading of the new and strange, do audiences actually want more of the same old "new and strange" exoticisms that appealed to their grandparents? In practice, translators usually accommodate the majority culture rather than defy its prejudices. As in other realms of communicative behavior, cooperation is preferable to conflict.[9] But sometimes conflict is unavoidable. After all, translators are in the business of transmitting foreign content, and what is foreign can be odd and shocking and thus provoke resistance. How much resistance there will be, and how it is to be dealt with, varies greatly from case to case.

I propose to explore the issue through a series of examples. One example that I choose from the Six Dynasties period has already been mentioned in my book *Translation as Citation*. Early translators of Buddhist texts could not really sidestep the fact that, in India at least, "monks do not bow to rulers." In India, it was already accepted as part of the reasoning behind the system of *varnas* or castes that Brahmins, by their monopoly on religious sacrifice and their abstention from war, were purer and more respectable than Kshatriyas, the ruler and soldier caste. Although Buddhists departed from many Hindu teachings, notably that of caste purity, Buddhist monks benefited from a tacit "grandfathering" of religiously exempt status on them and so were not obliged to show deference to kings. But compare that distinction with the universalist flavor of Chinese doctrines about perfect kingship developed in the Warring States period, when it was widely taken that the great problem of society was divided sovereignty: ideally, there must be "no land under heaven that is not the king's land; as far as the very edges of the earth, no man who is not the king's servant" 普天之下，莫非王土; 率土之濱，莫非王臣.[10] As Mencius put it, "The world's problems will be solved when it is brought under one rule" 天下惡乎定? 吾對曰: 定于一.[11] That is the theoretical justification for the existence of the empire. Clerics behaving as if they owed no obeisance to the civil authorities, as if they lived in a world of their own, were an intolerable exception to that universal rule. One would-be emperor, Huan Xuan 桓玄 (369–404), attempted to force the Buddhist sangha to recognize his authority and sent a message to that effect to the abbot Huiyuan (334–416), who replied with wit and erudition. I do not have the space here to go into the debate itself but will jump to its conclusion: beaten in his attempt to achieve dominance over the Buddhist community, Huan Xuan could only concede the power of translation to bring home extraordinary teachings from far away. Huiyuan asked: "If there were someone in this country who, bearing a royal commission, sought to penetrate the customs of remote regions, even those where ninefold translation is required, I ask you, would the king not offer him sustenance, official conveyance, and robes?" 有人於此奉宣時命遠通殊方九譯之俗，問王當資以糇糧錫以輿服不?

Huan Xuan's officials could only say "yes." By his own theory of kingship, Huan Xuan could not possibly, I suppose, admit the legitimacy of the monks' refusal to submit, so he made this gesture of acknowledgment to the translator's special abilities, as if the whole thing came down to a matter of translation.[12] And in a fictional sense it did. The ruler's assent to the Buddhist translation enterprise imagined the monastic community as residing at the edges of the empire, in a zone that could be communicated with only by nine relays of bilingual translators. To say so was to pretend to be unaware of the fact that thousands of Buddhists were living and building monasteries all over Six Dynasties China, or rather, to affirm that they held their tenure there only through the power of the foreign text. How powerful was that text, under these conditions?

Literary traditions tend, as did the tyrant Huan Xuan, to take their own standards as the ultimate in correctness and to demand that translated works pay homage to them by adhering to their rules. In his specific moment, Huiyuan was up to the challenge: his reply to Huan Xuan turned on ingenious interpretations of passages in *Zhuangzi*, *Lunyu*, and other classical Chinese source texts, which he showed he knew better than the officials did. What is sometimes called *geyi* 格義 interpretation, the selective deployment of passages from accepted classical texts in the service of spreading Buddhist ideas, turns on just this kind of clever repurposing, an adaptive use of old texts in new contexts. That is one translation strategy that I see being used again and again in Chinese literary history, and I call it "translation as citation": it's a matter of citing the *Yi jing*, for example, as if it had been written by the same authorities who wrote the Hebrew Bible, and updating the classic's meaning through a kind of conceptual pun. In a lesser degree, we see translators hasten to adopt the conventions and styles of Chinese literary writing, performing an elaborate masquerade like Matteo Ricci adopting the mannerisms of a Ming-dynasty *shanren* 山人 or hermit-sage.[13] Fidelity to the European originals was rarely the leading concern, and how should that surprise us, since hardly anyone in China could access those originals at the time those translations were done? The translation was going to be read if it spoke to a Chinese audience that had little or no knowledge of the Bible, Cicero, Aristotle, or whatever other source it drew on; without local appeal, it was dead on arrival. This strategy of camouflage, of hijacking, of slipping your meaning under the patronage of an already authoritative but unrelated classic, is what we might call a "weapon of the weak" in the struggle to gain acceptance for translated materials.[14] It subverts and appropriates, taking on the protective coloration of its environment and exchanging identities with what it imitates.

Where the need to adapt to the literary environment is felt most strongly, the properties that signal the foreignness of the foreign text are not particularly valued. In a famous passage, the great Buddhist scholar and abbot Dao'an 道安, around the year 360 of our era, wrote about the losses (shiben 失本) and the difficulties (buyi 不易) encountered when translating a foreign text—"translating from Hu into Qin" 譯胡為秦, as he put it. This passage, with its "five instances of loss from the source" and its "three difficulties," has been treated as a founding document of Chinese translation theory. Luo Xinzhang 羅新璋, for example, comments that Dao'an "strongly puts the case for accuracy. . . . His is absolutely the method of literal translation: demanding faithfulness and precision, taking care that no loss occur from the source" 力主矜慎 . . . 完全是直譯派的做法，務求忠實審慎，就兢于不失本.[15] But if we look more closely, we will find that Dao'an's preface is not actually about translation but about editing. Dao'an was apparently not a speaker of the "Hu language" (which might have been Pali, Sanskrit, or one of the several other languages through which Buddhist teachings were transmitted to China). But the preface shows that he is able to line up translated texts with their source texts, and thus to note discrepancies among them, without necessarily being able to interpret the sources. He mentions one text, brought to the Jin court as tribute by a Buddhist master from Turfan named Kumārabodhi 鳩摩羅跋提, that "consists of 420 leaves, said to contain twenty thousand slokas ['verses']. A sloka consists of thirty-two letters. The Hu number their classics and sutras. When counted up, there are in all 17,260 slokas [in this document]. When fragmentary passages of 27 letters have been accounted for, in all there are 552,475 letters" 獻胡大品一部，四百二牒言。二十千失盧。失盧三十二字。胡人數經法也。即審數之。凡十七千二百六十首盧。殘二十七字都并五十五萬二千四百七十五字.[16] A rough-and-ready quantitative analysis on the level of verses and sections in a foreign text is possible without knowledge of the foreign language. In the same way, if I were presented a bilingual legal document in Armenian and Georgian, though I can read neither, I could, approximately, tell if the two language-versions contained the same number of paragraphs and sentences. I would still have very little understanding of the document, but I could at least flag obvious problems about missing or added sections. Dao'an goes on to explain why discrepancies arise:

譯胡為秦，有五失本也。一者胡言盡倒，而使從秦，是一失本也。二者胡經尚質，秦人好文 ... 是二失本也。三者胡經委悉，至於歎詠，叮嚀反覆，或三或四，不嫌文煩 ... 四者胡有義說，正似亂辭，尋說、向說，文無以異，... 五者事以合成，將更傍及，反騰前辭，已乃後說，而悉除此，是五失本也。[17]

When translating from Hu languages to Chinese, five kinds of loss from the source (*shiben* 失本) may arise. One is when the Hu words are reversed and made to follow the Chinese word order.... The Hu sutras prize substance (*zhi* 質), but Chinese like pattern (*wen* 文).... [Adapting the text to Chinese taste] is the second kind of discrepancy. Third, the Hu sutras are verbose and go into sighs and exclamations. A moral may be repeated three and four times, without anyone feeling it tedious.... Fourth: the Hu text may have semantic notations that appear to be random verbiage, and if you seek a gloss you often find they simply repeat the text [and thus indicate that no one has understood the foreign expression].... The fifth is that sometimes, when some matter has already been thoroughly explained, the text recounts it again from another side, doubling back to the previous wording and laying it all out again; and removing this sort of thing is the fifth kind of discrepancy.[18]

By more clearly defining Dao'an's role as that of an editor, we can better understand his position on the so-called losses and difficulties: he is collating past translations, noting the gaps, and explaining the existence of those gaps by the difference in literary taste between Hu and Chinese publics. He remarks on the excesses of Hu literary style, not in the spirit of someone who thinks that the original is precious and must be retained at all costs, but with a relativist's awareness of different customs and different attitudes. His task as editor of the translated Buddhist corpus is guided by the need to ensure that the texts in that corpus will be both complete and consistent. To achieve this agreement, Dao'an advocates the practice of *he ben* 合本, "concordance among versions," which has often been taken to be a synonym of another phrase Dao'an uses, *anben er chuan* 案本而傳, "to transmit in accordance with the text(s)"; but again we must remember that comparison with the meaning of the foreign original is not in Dao'an's capacities; he simply seeks to use what he knows about the different translations of the same text to discover the passages that are missing in one or added to another, so that he can ensure that the text that comes out of his workshop will lack nothing.

To sum up, Dao'an's remarks on translation are issued from the receiving side of the transaction. We would not think of him as a translator today, if we mean by translator a person with bilingual abilities who restates in language B what someone has already said in language A. Dao'an's greatest influence on Buddhist translation, I think, lay in setting up standards and methods for compiling variants and combining those in a final text. Insofar as he was able to apply those methods across the whole of the Buddhist canon as it then existed, he created a new single-language library that exhibited high reliability, in the sense that we give that word today in testing and statistics—*reliability* as opposed to *validity*. (By "reliable" we mean that members of a group being examined will be more likely than not to give the same answer to a question; the word "valid" refers to the separate issue of whether that answer is actually correct.) If the different Chinese versions of a text agreed among themselves but the Indic original was not accurately reflected in those translations, Dao'an would have no way of discovering that discrepancy; their reliability would not equal validity. So, then, in a situation where the equivalence between a Sanskrit term and its Chinese corresponding terms could not be assessed on the basis of a bilingual acquaintance with Chinese and Sanskrit, because of the lack of bilingual subjects, Dao'an sought at least to ensure that the vocabulary of terms used in Chinese would be consistent enough that all Chinese Buddhists would be confident that they were talking about the same things. This is a good measure— it's essential, I would think, if you are founding a community of people who are to agree with one another in matters of metaphysical opinion that are beyond the scope of direct observation. The scale of operations matters. Dao'an in the late fourth century already had a vast library of Chinese texts to harmonize, but only a few foreign informants, and very little means of inspecting the so-called original texts (many of which must have been brought to China stored in memory, not in writing, by those foreign informants). The only way he could do that was by "translating without translating," if I may be permitted to lift a phrase from Bruce Lee.[19] That is, by editing.

If we remove from consideration the huge library of Buddhist texts translated or reconstituted from foreign languages, the archive of Chinese translation before the year 1800 shrinks considerably. If we take another step and put aside diplomatic communications, treaties, and other administrative documents addressed to or issued by foreign-language speakers, it shrinks yet further, and if we restrict ourselves to considering literary works, that is, documents of imagination, learning, or argumentation, translated from other languages into Chinese, we will have a slender sample to put against the immense library of Chinese texts. I wish in this way to put my subject in perspective, to show why it has so often been neglected, and to argue that the disproportion between native works and translated works in Chinese is a significant fact about Chinese literature, one that relates to other features of traditional Chinese culture that ought to be described, explained, and contextualized. Living as we do in one of Liang Qichao's "eras of translation," we may too easily assume that everyone has always lived in an era of translation, or that activities similar to translation, like Dao'an's editing projects, are translation when in fact they are subtly but irreducibly different. Against the contemporary tendency to inflate the term *translation* so as to portray every act of communication, every relationship, every intervention, every dialogue, every metaphor, every discovery as being in some way a translation, I prefer to keep the focus on linguistic difference and the specific modes of mediation between languages and their communities of speakers.[20] Nonetheless, I also think it is useful to have in mind the many types of cultural mediation that approximate translation, or do some of the work of translation, without quite being identical with it. Let us then draw a narrow boundary around translation understood as the rendering, by bilingual speakers and writers, of an original text into a similar text in a different language, and draw a wider boundary around the zone of mediation of cultural difference through all kinds of language-based resources, including editing, cross-media adaptation, and transcription. And let us, within those boundaries, specify the direction translation takes: translation inward, from foreign languages to Chinese, and translation outward, from Chinese into other idioms. All these differences are worth noticing. Knowing, or caring to know, which kind of mediation we are dealing with in a particular case will lead us to a clearer view of Chinese literary history and the cultural politics of Asia as a whole.

Mediation between different languages and communities can take many forms. There are translators; there are chains of translators, as Sima Qian's scenario of the "nine relays" suggests; there are institutions, like the protocols of monastic revision devised by

Dao'an to secure reliable versions of Buddhist texts imported by a variety of foreign informants; and not least, there are technologies, like the Chinese writing system or Arabic numerals, that create commensurabilities among separate linguistic communities. Chinese writing itself will prove both a tremendous enabler and a tremendous obliterator of translation.

When a sutra, recited or transcribed by a Sogdian or Khotanese informant, was paraphrased by a Chinese interpreter and taken down by a Chinese scribe, this translation inward would be followed by further transformations and rewritings that resulted in a satisfactory text in the Buddhist variant of literary Chinese. This Chinese text might very well be carried with the spread of Buddhism to a country where translation outward was now required, to give the literary Chinese text a vernacular rendition in spoken Vietnamese, Korean, Japanese, Uyghur, or some other idiom. "Reading in the vernacular" is a simple phrase standing for several stages of mediation and differences of competence. It is not far different from intralingual glossing, as when an old or difficult text is read aloud and interspersed with explanations that are more easily understood. Glossing of classical, specialized, and archaic texts must have occurred every day in schools, temples, and administrative offices across China. But not only across China:

> [John] Whitman says that "[v]ernacular glossing of Chinese texts was a linguistic habitus practiced throughout the non-Chinese speaking Sinosphere," and "literacy meant being able to read a text that looks to modern readers like . . . 'Chinese' out loud in the local language." Whitman convincingly argues that various glossing practices were integral to the development of true vernacular writing, at least in Korea and Japan. . . . Those who were highly skilled in Literary Sinitic could presumably translate into the vernacular and thus read aloud "on the fly." This would no doubt have been easier to do with shorter texts, especially those with formulaic structures: diplomatic missives, administrative orders, and the like. But longer and more

intricate texts . . . would have presented immense challenges to even the most learned scribes, let alone those with less training and experience.[21]

When a Chinese text was glossed in speech or writing for a public whose daily language was not Chinese, the vernacular rendition did not necessarily change the appearance of the characters; it changed, most manifestly, their sound values and, to some degree, their connotations and availability to readers of differing education levels. Oral and then graphic signals were added to the Chinese text in order to make it more readily understandable. In a further transformation, writers in the local scripts that had been invented in countries where literary Chinese was used internationally might use those scripts to paraphrase, allude to, re-create, or otherwise reinscribe texts that had originated in Chinese. Is vernacularization, defined in this way, a kind of translation? Yes and no; it is another case of not-quite translation, and to say exactly what it is we will need to imagine in more detail how it would take place. Consider a Korean literatus of the sixteenth century. He may have been trained from his earliest youth to recite, comment on, and write essays about Chinese classical texts. For him it is absolutely not a foreign language, although his pronunciation of the characters is not that of Beijing (and yet he may not know that). He no doubt also possesses the local script of Korea and can express the ideas of the Chinese Classics in that script as well. For that man's sister, unless she belongs to a family that goes to extremes in its embrace of the literati ideal, Chinese script is probably a foreign language and Korean script the available written form of her spoken language. When brother and sister talk together about the Cheng-Zhu interpretation of Mencius, as I am sure they must have done, how much of their conversation would we say *vernacularizes* the Chinese text and how much of it *translates* it? In this one imaginary pair of siblings, we find the extension of Chinese script to new territory (cross-border education in the original text of the Classics), translation outward (as when the content of those Classics is mediated for a nonreader of Chinese), and a certain kind of translation inward, if the Korean scholar should ever be moved by his sister's responses to draft an essay in Chinese that calls on ideas originally expressed by her in the Korean language.

Is our Korean scholar situated outside or inside China? For a good part of Chinese history, what we now know as Korea, that is, the overlapping kingdoms of Goguryeo, Paekche, Silla, and Chosŏn, were without a doubt territories of the "Eastern Alien Peoples" or *Dong yi* 東夷.[22] By the time of our imaginary Korean family, in the middle Ming, Korea was as well integrated into the Chinese cultural and political system as it could be without being an actual province; Koreans were known to sit for the examinations in China and to write poems and prose pieces that were included in Chinese anthologies. In the comprehensive *Liechao shiji* 列朝詩集 (1652) of Qian Qianyi 錢謙益 and Liu Rushi 柳如是, Korea was particularly well represented, with an aristocratic Korean woman, Hŏ Nansŏrhŏn 許蘭雪軒, attesting to the Chinese poetic language's power to transcend barriers of nationality and gender.[23] For several generations after the Qing invasion, as is well known, scholarly Koreans remained officially loyal to the Ming calendar and rituals and even went so far as to give their own country the name *xiao Zhonghua* ("little China").[24] I can well imagine that our Korean scholar would be indignant if we told him that his vernacularization of Mencius or Zhu Xi was a translation into a foreign language. "Foreign! Do you mean, barbaric?" Consideration of these facts must be fed into the question of just what place to give translation in the cultural traffic between China and Korea. For when we say translation, we are implying alienness, difference, failure to understand, a gap that must be overcome through the labor of translating; and the people on both sides of that gap may have differing estimations of how big the gap is. Denizens of the center may have one appreciation of what linguistic competence means, and denizens of the peripheries may have another; men may see it differently from women, members of different social classes may understand translation in their own ways, and so on. My advice at this point is not to seek a clear and univocal measure of what translation is, but to develop as many situated profiles of translation in context as we can, so as to delineate a whole field in all its varied shadings.

As so often, technology—here the technology of Chinese writing—disturbs typologies made by and for humans. The adoption of this technology renders moot the usual issues of equivalence. How do you say *ren* 仁 and *yi* 義 in Korean, or Japanese, or Vietnamese? How do you say *zhongyong* 中庸, *tianming* 天命, *sancongside* 三從四德, or any other tags and slogans of traditional morality?[25] In one sense, the question could be answered by repeating the characters in their local pronunciations, but that seemingly simple expedient sidesteps the question of the degree to which such terms may have become part of the language and culture of these and other non-Chinese but Chinese-influenced nations. Were we to say, on the one hand, that these units of meaning can *only* have originated in China and been exported to Japan, Korea, and Vietnam, we would be making an ethnocentric ethical claim; were we, on the other, to assert that the Chinese phrases merely came to give a new form to moral intuitions that preexisted Chinese literacy in those territories, we might bring comfort to local pride but at the same time seem to confirm the universality and inevitability of ideas that do, after all, as far as we know, have a particular place and time of origin. Both these ways of speaking seem to miss the mark. I hold it most probable and accurate to say that the terms of Chinese ethical discourse, like the terms of Chinese law, administration, technology, religion, and so forth, must have imposed themselves on and reconfigured some existing terms, but done so with the weight of words that came with an already powerfully developed system of implications and institutions. Although the actual stages of the adaptation are by now inaccessible to us, we can assume that rather than a translation as we usually conceive of it, namely, a proposed equivalence between terms in mutually distinct languages, what happened in the spread of Chinese writing and its related institutions to new territories was rather in the nature of an inscription: that is, an imposition on local material of an external form.[26]

In *The Genesis of East Asia*, Charles Holcombe makes the case for China's possessing an "empire of ideas" over its neighbors through the spread of its written characters: "*Kanji* [漢字, Chinese characters] are tied inextricably to a particular set of ideas—to a specific vocabulary or 'ideology.' . . . The use of *kanji* throughout East Asia therefore creates an 'empire of ideas,' which simultaneously reinforces and circulates Chinese concepts and excludes other ideas or at least makes their expression difficult. For this reason, they are the most powerful glue that could possibly bind together East Asia."[27]

Yes, I would say, but "ideas" seem to me a vague and weightless sort of thing. It was an empire of words, concepts, rules, institutions, standards, measures, rituals, behaviors, texts, and relationships, held together by moral and logical obligation and if necessary by force. Here is an illustration. In the year 590, after quelling and absorbing the Chen empire and thus reunifying northern and southern China for the first time in three hundred years, Emperor Wen of the Sui 隋文帝 turned his attention to his northern frontiers, in particular to the tributary state of Gaogouli/Goguryeo, the biggest of the Korean kingdoms, which had begun preparing defenses against a possible Sui invasion while keeping up a diplomatic pretense of loyalty. Emperor Wen sent the Goguryeo king a strongly worded letter that read in part:

朕受天命, 愛育率土, 委王海隅, 宣揚朝化, 欲使圓首方足, 各遂其心。王每遣使人, 歲常朝貢, 雖稱籓附, 誠節未盡。王既人臣, 須同朕德, 而乃驅逼靺鞨, 固禁契丹。諸籓頓顙, 爲我臣妾, 忿善人之慕義, 何毒害之情深乎? 太府工人, 其數不少, 王必須之, 自可聞奏。昔年潛行財貨, 利動小人, 私將弩手, 逃竄下國。... 朕於蒼生, 悉如赤子, 賜王土宇, 授王官爵, 深恩殊澤, 彰著遐邇。... 賜王土宇, 授王官爵, 深恩殊澤, 彰著遐邇。... 今日以后, 必須改革。... 彼之一方, 雖地狹人少, 然普天之下, 皆為朕臣。[28]

Having received the Mandate of Heaven, We cherish and maintain the lands in our care, appointing subordinate kings to supervise borders and seas and to carry out the transforming mission of Our dynasty, so that all humanity may live in happiness. But in the several instances where you have sent emissaries, and in your ordinary yearly tribute offerings, though you have avowed fealty as a bulwark state, your obligations of sincerity have not been fully carried out. As Our subordinate, you are to lend yourself to Our prestige; yet you have harassed the Mohe tribesmen and refused passage to the Khitans.[29] The many bulwark states must bow their heads, agreeing to serve Us as ministers and handmaidens. But when someone displays anger toward the laudable intentions of good men—how deep a desire to do evil must this betoken! The craftsmen in Our imperial workshops are by no means few; if you indeed had need of them, you had only to address a memorial to Us. In recent years you have made surreptitious use of your wealth to stir up petty people desiring gain. You have even induced crossbow-makers to sneak over the borders into your minor kingdom. . . . We look upon humankind with the tenderness of an infant's caretaker.[30] We have granted you lands to inhabit and bestowed on you official ranks. Our deep grace and extraordinary bounty toward you are known far and near. . . . From today forward there must be a change, there must be reform. . . . Your country is small and its population scanty, but under the whole of heaven, none but is Our subject.

It seems to me that the language of international relations wielded by Emperor Wen's officials predetermines the outcome of the dialogue. The terms themselves are so heavily loaded with connotations that worked in the center's interests (the center being here presented as the source of virtue, beneficence, justice, and peace) that it is hard to imagine framing a ritually correct answer that would not be a capitulation. The means of communication shapes the content of any possible reply. Merely to participate in the Chinese written language presumed acceptance of a set of power relations and possible subject positions that were not easily open to renegotiation.

Was the letter effective? According to the *Sui shu*, "when Tang"— the king's personal name, the use of which is a signal of delegitimation by the historian—"had received this letter, he was terrified, and begged forgiveness in the humblest terms. Shortly thereafter he fell ill and died" 湯得書惶恐，將奉表陳謝，會病卒.[31] This telling makes it seem that the Sui dynasty's bark was sufficient, without a bite.

Or that it should have been, for when the Sui under their next emperor, Yangdi 隋煬帝, mounted an invasion of Goguryeo along the Liao River in 612, they were thoroughly defeated. Goguryeo kept its territory, and the Sui dynasty, exhausted by imperial overreach, collapsed a few years later. This outcome has not prevented mainland Chinese scholars from taking Sui Wendi's letter at its word and asserting that Goguryeo was actually a Chinese territory, provoking predictable backlash from Korean historians.[32]

A further testimony to the power of Chinese writing is that the earliest recorded history of all the peoples of the area is to be found not in the local languages of the people concerned but in the ethnographic sections of the Chinese dynastic histories, with all the biases and selectivity that one might expect. For example, the description of Goguryeo national character preceding the copy of Emperor Wen's letter emphasizes customs that violate Chinese expectations of ritual correctness: there fathers and sons bathe together in rivers; when a man pleases a woman, the two run off together, and it is only later that the man's household seals the union by sending a gift of pigs and liquor; a great many spirits and ghosts are worshipped indiscriminately.[33] It is not surprising, then, that the king of such a country "misunderstood" his place.

Peter Kornicki, Zev Handel, and Kin Bunkyō have recently written histories of the international circulation of the Chinese writing system, including the vernacular reading of Chinese in other languages such as Korean, Japanese, Vietnamese, and Tangut, and the development of new scripts initially taking

Chinese script as their basis.[34] In those areas a script diglossia might thus be created, with Chinese letters serving for high culture and international communication and a derivative, local script serving for strictly local communication with often less prestigious content. This stratified bilingualism, vernaculars being written and spoken alongside an international written language, is nicely exemplified by a sequence of poems from the *Man'yōshū* attributed to the members of a Japanese embassy to the kingdom of Silla on the Korean peninsula. Their exchanges took place in the year 736. The envoys were men of literary culture who wrote in Chinese, of course, when dealing with their Korean counterparts. An ambassador might present a poem like this one, adorned with suitable *Shijing* allusions, at the farewell banquet:

新知未幾日，
送別何依依 . . .
相顧鳴鹿爵，
相送使人歸．

New friends just met,
we find parting hard to bear. . . .
Exchanging glances, we chant the "Deer Cry" song and lift
     our cups,
sending the envoys homeward.[35]

Moreover, the envoys wrote poems in Japanese about the pains of parting and the longing for home, using the Chinese character-set as a sort of syllabary and not neglecting to allude to Chinese canonical literature in their verses. One such *Man'yōshū* poem appears below in its several guises—sinographic transliteration on the left, romanization on the right, and in the middle a *hiragana* transcription with the semantically referenced *kanji* indicated:

安麻等夫也	あま(天)と(飛)ぶや	amatobuya
可里乎都可比尔	かり(雁)をつかひ(使)に	kariwotsukahini
衣弖之可母	え(得)てしかも	eteshikamo
奈良能弥夜故尔	なら(奈良)のみやこ(都)に	naranomiyakoni
許登都ん夜良武	ことつ(言告)げや(遣)らむ	kototsugeyaramu[36]

Would that I had
a goose for a messenger
to course across the sky!
I would send tidings
to the Nara capital.[37]

The two prefaces supplied by Ki no Yoshimochi 紀淑望 and Ki no Tsurayuki 紀貫之 for the *Kokin[waka]shū* 古今和歌集 (*Anthology of Waka Poems, Ancient and Modern*), around the year 900, offer another framing of the conditions of this bilateral or biliteral sensibility. Although the collection consists of *waka* poems in Japanese, Yoshimochi's preface in Chinese directly imitates the preface to the Chinese *Book of Songs* (*Shijing* 詩經) and argues that Japanese vernacular poetry matches in every way the standards of that timeless Chinese work. Tsurayuki's preface in Japanese argues that *waka* poets are even better than Chinese poets at expressing their uniquely acute feelings. Although, as Timothy Wixted puts it, "there is no new critical theory in the *Kokinshū* prefaces . . . the concrete vocabulary of the applied criticism in the prefaces evidences a sensibility that is not subject to Chinese models."[38] This brings out rather nicely the difference between an acquired semantic framework—the result of an imposition or inscription of a written culture from elsewhere—and the sometimes unruly matter to which the framework might be applied. Naturally some Japanese writers wrote perfectly competent and correct Chinese verses and were proud to have them anthologized alongside the work of Chinese authors. But that is the way a peripheral subject is expected to respond to the center. For whom were the *Kokinshū* prefaces written? Certainly not for a Chinese audience: communication with China was rare, and no Chinese reader at the time would have made the effort to learn Japanese in order to read *waka* poetry.[39] Yoshimochi's Chinese preface addresses other Japanese competent in Chinese, people who had internalized the standards of Chinese poetry and possibly needed to be persuaded that poems in Japanese were in any way significant, or that Japanese could be a legitimate language for poetry.

Tsurayuki's preface relies for its authority on exactly the same Chinese sources as does Yoshimochi's but promises that the poetry of Japan will surpass China's in a language and a form all its own. On what conditions, though, can Tsurayuki's claim be verified by monolingual readers of Chinese? The masterpieces of Heian literature—the *Tale of Genji*, *The Pillow Book*, and the like— would not be translated into Chinese until the second half of the twentieth century.

A great deal of recent translation theory has turned on the position of English, or Global English. It is seen as both enabling and repressing international communication, and constraining the terms in which ideas can be circulated. I feel that these discussions are hobbled by the failure to articulate something adequately general. What *in general* is the role of a dominant monolingual culture? If English were to vanish from the face of the earth tomorrow, would the problem of imperial monolingualism vanish with it? What does a dominant language make happen? How do those outside that language respond to it and negotiate with it? Having a theory, as opposed to having a grievance, means seeing causes and effects, rights and wrongs, in more than one context, and submitting the case to the judgment of a public more widely distributed in both space and time. Claims of cultural uniqueness both appeal to and retreat from the universal. What is involved in demanding a hearing for nondominant cultures, in general? If the case for the value of a minority culture is to be made at all, it must be made in terms alien to it, universalizing terms—which may seem to lead us into paradox. Let us call it the Paradox of Forums. Addressing this paradox, the next chapter will take the examination of translated literature in Asia closer to its attested beginnings by asking, "Can the Barbarians Sing?"

2

Can the Barbarians Sing?

四夷作樂乎?

HOWEVER WE DEFINE CHINA—and there are many answers to
that question on offer these days, in bookstores, in journals, and on
the political stage—it has always been multicultural; that is, it has
accommodated the contact of different ways of life maintained by
groups that thought of themselves as different from each other.[1] It
has been multilingual, too, however you define that, and its inhabitants have situated themselves in different histories, despite cease-
less efforts at centralization. That is obvious to us, but it was a problem for the classical scholars of the early Han court. The *Collected
Discussions in the White Tiger Hall* (*Baihu tongyi* 白虎通義), compiled after 79 CE, include a discussion of the virtues of music,
framed, as in the writings of Xunzi 荀子 and the *Li ji* 禮記 (Records
of ritual), as a counterpart to ritual. As Xunzi put it: ritual distinguishes, but music brings together.[2] Ritual establishes hierarchies,
but music creates feelings of commonality. Ritual without music
becomes dry and sterile; music without ritual becomes a chaotic
indulgence. Thus, through the logic of serial redefinition and repeated parallelism characteristic of Warring States and Han sys-
tematizing thought, music is established among the institutions
that realize the ideal community envisioned by the long-ago sages.
Given that understanding of the effects of music, however, a problem crops up in the Classics. The *Rituals of Zhou* 周禮, for example,

state that "music of the four alien tribes" was performed during court ceremonies. (I am using "alien" as a provisional translation for *yi* 夷, in preference to the overloaded term *barbarian*; at times I will just write *yi*.) The wording is: "The Dīlóu takes charge of the Four Alien Tribes' music and accompanies it with sung words. At the sacrifice, he is to blow and sing it, and at banquets likewise" 鞮鞻氏: 掌四夷之樂與其聲歌。祭祀, 則吹而歌之; 燕, 亦如之.[3] *Dilou* (like its near-equivalent *didi* 狄鞮) is a word found only in situations of foreign contact, and the "leather" radical on the left side of both characters connotes something rough and outdoorsy—giving in all a barbaric impression.[4] And yet the text suggests that in the ideal realm of the founding Zhou, this exotic word, *dilou*, was the title of an official specially assigned to perpetuate the art of foreign music. In response to such passages highlighting "barbarian" music, the *Baihu tong* authors cite the *Yue yuanyu* 樂元語 (Authoritative discourses on music), a lost work still current in the Han, to correct the earlier classic:

所以作四夷之樂何? 德廣及之也。 ... 《樂元語》曰: 「受命而六樂。樂先王之樂, 明有法也; 與其所自作, 明有制; 興四夷之樂, 明德廣及之也。」[5]

What is the reason for having the "music of the four alien tribes" performed?—[To show that] the royal virtue had spread even to them. . . . The *Yue yuanyu* says: "A ruler who has received the Mandate causes six kinds of music to be performed. The music of the Former Kings is performed to show his legitimacy. Then he has music from his own reign performed, in order to display his instituting power. Thereafter he has music of the Four Yi performed, in order to show that his virtue extends even to them."

There are some further specifications about the differences among these sorts of music:

故南夷之樂曰《兜》, 西夷之樂曰《禁》, 北夷之樂曰《昧》, 東夷之樂曰《離》。 合歡之樂人舞於堂, 四夷之樂陳於右, 先王所以得之, 順命重始也。 《樂元語》曰: 「東夷之樂持矛舞, 助時

生也；南夷之樂持羽舞，助時養也；西夷之樂持戟舞，助時煞
也。」北夷之樂持干舞，助時藏也。誰制夷狄之樂？以為先
聖王也。先王惟行道德，和調陰陽，覆被夷狄，故夷狄安
樂，來朝中國，於是作樂樂之。[6]

Thus the music of the Southern Yi is called "Dou"; the music of
the Western Yi is called "Jin"; the music of the Northern Yi is
called "Mei"; the music of the Eastern Yi is called "Li." The musicians perform celebratory music in the hall; the music of the
Four Aliens is kept outside and to the right. [The sovereign] has
received music from the Former Kings, and as a sign of perpetuat-
ing the Mandate causes it to be begun again. . . . The *Yue yuanyu*
says: "The music of the Eastern Yi is danced with spears; it accompanies timely sprouting. The music of the Southern Yi is
danced with feathers; it accompanies timely growth. The music of
the Western Yi is danced with halberds; it accompanies timely
ripening. The music of the Northern Yi is danced with shields; it
accompanies timely harvest."—If the Northern Yi dance with
shields to aid in the harvest, who made the music for the Yi and
Di tribes?—It is the doing of the former Sage Kings. The Former
Kings practiced the Way and virtue and harmonized yin and yang;
this came to cover even the Yi and Di. Thereupon the Yi and Di,
being joyful and at peace, came to pay homage in the Central
States, and [the Kings] made music to gladden them withal.

As Yu Siu-wah has observed, the elaboration on the regional
types of music serves to arrange the barbaric states in a symmetrical pattern centered on the Zhou king, a kind of mandala and calendar wherein the foreign tribes each have a season, but the whole
year remains the property of the center; they revolve around the
central monarch, as elements of a conceptual Hall of Lights or
mingtang 明堂. The qualities of each of the outer quadrants are
specific to that quadrant and negate those of the quadrant opposite to it. Only the center accommodates each quality in turn, as
the changing seasons of the year bring one or another quadrant
into closer relation with the Son of Heaven, who sits at the pivot

<table>
<tr><td></td><td>Northern Di:
Mei 昧</td><td></td></tr>
<tr><td>Western Rong:
Jin 禁</td><td>**Zhou Sovereign** 周天子</td><td>Eastern Yi:
Li 離</td></tr>
<tr><td></td><td>Southern Man:
Dou 兆</td><td></td></tr>
</table>

Illustration adapted from Yu Siu-wah, "Zhongguo yinyue de bianyuan"

of it all. Position (where a thing is) amounts to essence (what kind of thing it is).

Moreover, in a clinching move on the part of the *Baihu tong* authors, the Yi and Di may have music, but it isn't really theirs; they have it as a gift from the people who invented culture, namely, Yao, Shun, Yu, Zhou Gong, and the other heroes of the Central States and the empire. The reason has to do ultimately with the capacities of the different populations:

> 夷狄質, 不如中國文, 但隨物名之耳, 故百王不易。王者制夷狄樂, 不制夷狄禮何? 以為禮者, 身當履而行之, 夷狄之人不能行禮; 樂者, 聖人作為以樂之耳, 故有夷狄樂也。誰為舞者? 以為使中國之人。何以言之? 夷狄之人禮不備, 恐有過誤也。作之門外者何? 夷在外, 故就之也。夷狄無禮義, 不在內。[7]

The Yi and Di are crude; they lack the refinement of the Central States; the names given to them and their music simply follow their material characteristics, and though a hundred reigns may come and go, these names do not change. [The contrast is with Chinese ritual custom of refashioning and renaming institutions to suit each new dynasty.]—When the Kings made [or ordered] Yi and Di music, did they not also make Yi and Di rituals?—[No,] because rituals are a precedent to be followed with one's person, and the Yi and Di people are incapable of performing a ritual; music, on the other hand, is something that the Sages made to give them pleasure, and as a result there is Yi and Di music [but no corresponding ritual].—And who performs the dance? It must be performed by people who come on mission to the Central States.—Why so?—The Yi and Di are incapable of ritual, and [were they to attempt to participate in court ritual] it is to be feared that there would be flaws and misunderstandings [so dance is sufficient].—Why do they make music from outside the gate [of the palace]?—The Yi are outside, that is their destination. Being people without understanding of ritual, the Yi and Di must remain outside the gate.

Ritual inferiority is the condition on which some bits of Yi and Di culture are allowed to approach the palace, that central showplace: not as a coequal or competitive culture, but as an incomplete and unmeaning outward show, good enough for foreigners but never the real thing, and (at least in the Han-dynasty interpretation) kept on the threshold, not brought in. A commentary to the *Zhou li* elaborates:

禮者，所以均中國也。即為夷禮，恐夷人不能隨中國禮也。故春秋于夷狄不備責，諸夏有即夷禮者，即夷之也。[8]

The Rites are used for the regulation of the Central States. When rituals were concocted for the Yi, it was feared that Yi people were incapable of following the Rites used by the Central States. This is why the *Chunqiu* [*Spring and Autumn Annals*] never imposes the full burden of ritual observations on the Yi and Di. But if ever people of Xia [more or less, "Chinese"] descent engage in alien rituals, that is reason for the *Chunqiu* to treat them as aliens.

Han Yu 韓愈 paraphrases this passage more succinctly:

孔子之作《春秋》也，諸侯用夷禮則夷之，進於中國則中國之。[9]

When Confucius composed the *Spring and Autumn Annals,* wherever the feudal lords adopted alien rites he treated them as aliens; wherever they approximated the rites of the Central States, he treated them as belonging to the Central States.

Membership in the culture of the Central States is by no means guaranteed by birth or residence; it depends on conformity to a pattern, and that pattern, over the course of centuries, condenses around a single figure. As the *Zhongyong* 中庸 puts it: 非天子，不議禮，不制度，不考文。今天下車同軌，書同文，行同倫 "To no one but the Son of Heaven does it belong to order ceremonies, to fix the measures, and to determine the written characters. Now, throughout the world, cart-tracks are all of one width; all writing is with the same characters; and for conduct there are the same rules."[10] Political centralization and cultural exclusivity go hand in hand.

With any account of cultural creation in imperial China, we need to carefully distinguish the expressive and normative strands, the statement of how things are and the statement of how things ought to be. These two things are not the same; they don't quite contradict each other, though they can overlay each other and confuse the unwary observer. It may absolutely not be the fact that the Yi and Di music was given them by Yao and Shun, or the Duke of Zhou; its not being the case does not hinder it from being, for a certain kind of official aesthetics, what ought to have been the case; and official aesthetics is always ready to enforce the doctrine that the normative is the actual. The power to set norms derives from the creative act of the Former Kings. This is entirely in the spirit of Xunzi, who said, five hundred years before the *Baihu tong*, "In ancient times, the sage kings saw that because people's nature is bad, they were deviant, dangerous and not correct, unruly, chaotic, and not well ordered. Therefore, for their sake the sage kings set up ritual and loyalty, and established proper models and measures" 古者聖王以人性惡，以為偏險而不正，悖亂而不治，是以為之起禮義，制法度。[11] Who could possibly be more deviant, dangerous, incorrect, unruly, and chaotic than aliens and barbarians?

So they must be excluded from the provision of music, inasmuch as proper music reflects ritual, and bad music corrupts the public.

We need to pause for a moment and work out the meaning of this term *yi* 夷, "alien" or "barbarian." Who or what is a *yi*? The designation is a shifting one over the three thousand years of its usage, but there are a few constants. *Yi* (often correlated with *fang* 方, "boundary" in oracle-bone writings) are outsiders as seen from within the Chinese cultural space. Some *yi* are nomads and live primarily from animal husbandry; others are hillside gardeners and gatherers. They have different customs from the Central States, and they speak incomprehensible languages, requiring translators to mediate. Usually, they do not have writing or walled cities. Numerical epithets like *duofang* 多方 (the many boundary-people), *jiu yi* 九夷 (the nine *yi*), and *bai yi* 百夷 (the hundred *yi*) point to their decentralized political organization and their confusing multiplicity. An epithet like *si yi* 四夷 (the four *yi*) or *si fang* 四方 (the four *fang*) tries, in compensation, to put them in a system, to control them verbally, to define them as an array around the center. The difference marked in such words is hierarchical. Using the designation *yi* has the effect of excluding the people referred to from the realm of manners, morals, reason, ritual, music, *li*, and *wen*.

Some years ago Lydia Liu examined the use the colonial British made of the term *yi* in their early diplomatic communications with the Qing government and observed that it functioned as a "super-sign," not just a word with a meaning that could be agreed on by participants in a conversation but a word that became the stakes of the whole conversation itself.[12] In the 1840s the British insisted that *yi* was an insulting term and demanded, in the Unequal Treaty that concluded the first Opium War, that it be excluded from future diplomatic communications. I agree with Liu here that the British were using *yi* in bad faith, as a pretext for stirring up conflict when they thought it was in their interest to do so, but that doesn't mean that everything said then, before, and since about *yi* was wrong and that we should therefore believe the opposite, that *yi* was a perfectly inoffensive and relative term. Vietnamese envoys in the Ming dynasty were once outraged at being put up at a "*yi* hostel"; they protested that they were no *yi* but part of the cultural efflorescence of the Hua 華.[13] When a group formerly considered *yi*, the Manchus, began to rule over China, the employ of the designation became a delicate matter. Imperial edicts and imperially sponsored compilations tested rival interpretations of the word: as geographical designation, as ethnic label, as term of moral condemnation. Venerable texts were censored and policy documents withdrawn from circulation as varying interests were weighed.[14]

The term's degree of offensiveness may be up to evaluation case by case, but relative it certainly is not. Unlike mere place markers such as *bi* and *ci* or *nei* and *wai* ("that," "this," "inner," "outer"), *yi* is not convertible. You can say that a native is foreign to a foreigner, and vice versa, but you can't say that a Chinese is *yi* to a foreigner, that is, to a person who is *yi*. There is no *yi* of *yi*. (Thus the translation as "foreign" loses much of the word's specificity of reference.) *Yi* is a word the meaning of which depends on its use within a particular language game.[15] Outside that game, it doesn't generalize. It would be straining the semantics to say that Kazakhs, for example, are *yi* to Russians; there's too much Chinese domain-specificity involved to allow any such wider application.

But what kind of difference does *yi* indicate? It may look like ethnic or racial difference, though we need to be careful about the danger of projecting backward in time concepts that were unavailable to our predecessors. Methods of classification of human beings are constantly being revised. One recognition of this mutability is the argument from the venerable philosophical text *Mencius*, cited again and again over the centuries, that far from being a permanent status, *yi* is a way of behaving, a cultural category rather than a nationality or an ancestry. The sage-king Shun (traditionally dated to the twenty-third century BCE) and King Wen of the Zhou dynasty (eleventh century BCE), those creators of Chinese culture, were originally *yi* from the Eastern and Western regions, respectively: "Shun was born at Zhufeng . . . thus he was an Eastern Yi. King Wen was born at Qizhou ... thus he was a Western Yi. ... But the policies that they caused to be adopted in the Central States, if you compare them, are like the two halves of a tally. The earlier and the later sage are as one in their standards" 舜生於諸馮 ... 東夷之人也。文王生於岐周 ... 西夷之人也。 ... 得志行乎中國，若合符節。先聖後聖，其揆一也。[16] Neither status nor origin mattered much to Mencius; civilizational action was what counted.

The one perduring thing about the label *yi* is not its meaning but its effect: the act of pronouncing difference. The objects to which that judgment of difference is applied can change over time (as when populations become Sinicized, or alien customs are adopted). *Yi* is a term with a moving horizon of applicability. But as an "actor category," *yi* can be wielded as if it were a permanent, inborn identity, as when Jiang Tong 江統 in the Western Jin (fourth century CE) summarized a number of traditional distinctions in order to mark off the *yi* and ask that they be expelled as a danger to the Central Realm:

以其言語不通，贄幣不同，法俗詭異，種類乖殊；或居絕域之外，山河之表，崎嶇川谷阻險之地，與中國壤斷土隔，不相侵涉，賦役不及，正朔不加，故曰「天子有道，守在四夷」。[17]

On account of their language being incomprehensible, their means of exchange different, their laws and customs awkward and strange, their race is remote from ours. Some live in the distant regions, others on the edges of mountains and rivers, in steep and inaccessible crags and valleys, at a distance from the soil of the Central States. They do not mix with us. They do not pay tax or offer corvée labor, they do not follow the [imperial] calendar, and so it is said that "when the Son of Heaven maintains the Way, we have the Four Yi as a barrier."

Jiang Tong's insistence on an irreducible difference is just one phase of a relationship that endured over millennia. Recent research like that of Nicola Di Cosmo and Tamara Chin shows how influential the relationships between Hua and various groups designated Yi were over the course of Chinese history, how they varied, and what groups took an interest in framing that relationship in one or another way.[18] I surmise that the cultural exclusivity expressed by the *Baihu tong* and Jiang Tong's essay, whatever its purported basis in fact, is a typical move in struggles for authority among policy groups and schools of thought at times when outsiders were considered a threat. Moreover, the persistence of that view on the superiority of the culture of the Central States indexes the permanent interests of the *wenren* 文人 (literati) who maintained that culture and drew from it their intellectual and social resources. As Erica Fox Brindley observes in her study of the Yue 越, "Ancient thinkers who leaned in the direction of strong traditionalist Ru [Confucian] values and norms sometimes spoke of cultural interactions in terms of purely one-way civilizing projects—through the concept of 'educational reform' (*jiao hua* 教化) . . . and goals."[19] Thus if we are looking mainly at the archive of *wenxue* 文學, of poetry and historiography and aesthetic theory, we should not expect to find many documents treating *yi* as fully human culture-creators.

Central and alien identities motivate gestures of opening and closure. Thus, in the days of the Zhou, the music of exotic peoples, played at court, was a rare commodity that declared the glory and influence of the royal house. Precisely because it came from far away and was imbued with otherness, it was good and valuable. By Han times, however, that exotic eclecticism was under attack by the purists at court whose voice dominates in the *Baihu tong*. Hence, I think, the stiffening of the opposition between *Zhuxia* and *Yi* among the court Confucians who speak in the *Baihu tong*, and the projection of imperial autocratic cultural authority back into the Zhou past that we see in the *Zhongyong*'s statement about the Son of Heaven determining the rites and unifying the written characters. That kind of centralization could not be declared as a fact by someone living at the time of Zisi

子思, the supposed author of the *Zhongyong*, whose dates are thought to be 481–401 BCE; it was a remarkable and radical proposal when put forth by Li Si 李斯 shortly after the founding of the empire in 221 BCE, so the *Zhongyong* passage must be indulging in a retrospective or idealizing anachronism, seeking legitimation in the late-Zhou past for a Qin or Han policy. Ritual, music, letters, and all other means of social interchange must come from the hands of the sage king. Other and lesser beings can only receive what the sage king has graciously bestowed. Though the *Zhongyong* passage carries this centralization and personalization to an extreme (all standards emanating from the decisions of the One Man), we see a milder form of the same impulse in the *Baihu tong*'s refusal of cultural initiative to the barbarians. They won't even have their own music, by the *Baihu tong*'s account of things. Culture, or *wen* 文, belongs to the people of the Central States. To put a bit of a contemporary spin on the matter, I see the *Baihu tong* authors as the sort of guardians of cultural identity who are always on the defensive, always fearful of any invasion of otherness and unwilling to acknowledge the debts their culture owes to others that it has chewed up and digested in the course of its development.

Can a barbarian sing?[20] Is there such a thing as Yi and Di music, or would admitting the Yi and Di to the ranks of music creators not subvert the whole division between culture and nonculture on which the ideology of centralized empire depends? Can a barbarian exhibit *wen* or refinement, that property reserved, in this admittedly ethnocentric discourse, to the people of the Central States?

The conditions of acceptance were not always so strict. Consider this account from Liu Xiang's *Shuo yuan* 說苑 (Garden of persuasions) of an event dated (perhaps legendarily) to the sixth century BCE. A nobleman from the state of Chu 楚, the Duke of E, Zixi 鄂君子皙, was out on a boating excursion and heard one of the boatmen singing:

濫兮抃草濫 *Lan xi bian cao lan*[21]
予昌枑澤予昌州 *Yu chang heng ze yu chang zhou*
州鵮州焉乎秦胥胥 *Zhou kan zhou yan hu qin xu xu*
縵予乎昭澶秦踰 *Man yu hu zhao tan qin yu*
滲惿隨河湖。 *Zhen ti sui he hu.*

鄂君子皙曰：『吾不知越歌，子試為我楚說之。』於是乃召
越譯，乃楚說之曰：

Zixi, Duke of E, said: "I do not understand this Yue song, please
try to say it to me in Chu [language]." Thereupon they called
for a Yue translator, and rendered it in Chu thus:

『今夕何夕兮，搴中洲流，
今日何日兮，得與王子同舟。
蒙羞被好兮，不訾詬恥，
心幾頑而不絕兮，得知王子。
山有木兮木有枝，心說君兮君不知。』

What night is tonight, that I take the boat to the middle of
 the stream?
What day is today, that I get to accompany my prince on
 the boat?
Ignorant and shy, I have hidden my affection, but now I do
 not fear being exposed or denounced.
Longing fills my heart and has no end; I can now be
 acquainted with my prince.
Mountains bear trees, trees bear branches; my heart
 rejoices in my lord, but he is not aware.

於是鄂君子皙乃擒脩袂，行而擁之，舉繡被而覆之。

At this, Zixi, Duke of E, stretched out his long sleeves, walked
over and embraced him, then lifted up his embroidered cape
and covered him with it.[22]

 The poem is the only surviving extended document in the
extinct language of Yue 越, once an important kingdom in

southeastern coastal China, inhabited by the "Bai Yue" 百越 or "Hundred Yue." Zhengzhang Shangfang's reinterpretation finds that the ancient Yue words as represented here appear to be cognate with Thai and Burmese; thus, at least in terms of language families, ancient Yue is not a "dialect" (a bothersome word) of Chinese at all. As the population and administration of the Central States expanded southwards the speakers of the Yue language presumably had to choose between assimilating and retreating southward. In any case, the song of the boatman as transcribed here displays its alien quality with exuberance—it is rare for a Han-dynasty author to quote a foreign text this long in the original. By including it among his examples of "deft persuasion," Liu Xiang—a dweller in the capital, a consummate insider, and, with his imperial surname, as representative a figure of centralized culture as one could wish—demonstrates the power of words, even when the words are incomprehensible and they are sung by a humble oarsman from Yue, who therefore belongs among the Dong Yi. His words, translated, gain the oarsman the companionship and appreciation of his social superior. At the date Liu Xiang assigns the anecdote (some six hundred years anterior to his present), both Chu and Yue would have counted as territories alien to the Zhou polity and its rituals. The barbarian sings! Translation brings the sincerity of his utterance into the ambit of what can be known by speakers of (what we call) Chinese. In it, the Duke can hear echoes of both the northern *Shijing* and the southern *Songs of Chu*, a recognition that calls the exotic utterance back into the universalized traditions of the Han.[23]

Another direct transcription of foreign song appears in *Hou Han shu*. Around the year 60 of our era, a young official eager to make a name for himself, Zhu Fu 朱輔, was appointed to the post of governor of Yizhou 益州, a vast territory in the Southwest. He was so successful at "proclaiming the greatness of the Han and winning the loyalty of distant and alien peoples" 宣示漢德，威懷遠夷 that members of the Bailang, Panmu, and Tangcu 白狼，槃木，唐菆 tribes, numbering as many as six million, came wishing to pay tribute and become subjects of the Han emperor. Zhu Fu wrote a memorial to accompany a delegation of representatives, departing to the capital to make their request. They were escorted by officials carrying three songs that the Bailang had composed, in a transcription of the foreign original as well as a translation into Chinese. "In the time of the Sage-Kings," said Zhu Fu in his letter of transmittal, "it was the custom to dance the music of the Four Alien Tribes. Perhaps [that time has come around again and] the songs I enclose herewith will supply a new example of the same" 昔在聖帝，舞四夷之樂。今之所上，庶備其一.[24]

The poems must have pleased the Han emperor. The first one, the "Song of Distant Aliens Rejoicing in Virtue" 遠夷樂德歌, reads:

大漢是治，與天合意。吏譯平端，不從我來。
聞風向化，所見奇異。多賜贈布，甘美酒食。
昌樂肉飛，屈申悉備。蠻夷貧薄，無所報嗣。
願主長壽，子孫昌熾。

In South Coblin's translation:

The great Han is in good order,
Together with Heaven it unites its intention.
The officials and translators are just and upright,
They did not, pursuing us, cause us to come.
Having heard the customs and faced toward the civilizing
    influences,
What we have seen is wonderful.
They have generously given us silk cloth
And sweet and fine wine and food.
In splendid happiness we are elated;
Whether we are declining or advancing, in all cases we are
    provided for.
We, the barbarians, being poor and thin,
Have nothing to give in repayment.
We wish for the ruler longevity
And that his sons and grandsons shall be splendid and
    glorious.[25]

This is exactly how and what the barbarian is supposed to sing. Under such conditions, including the music of the Four Alien Tribes as part of an imperial court ceremony is not bothersome, as it seems to have been to the *Baihu tong* debaters. But now a new puzzle arises: if a group of Yi (and a consequential group, as we see from the *History of the Later Han*: some six million individuals) asks to be included in the Chinese nation, are they still considered Yi? Are their descendants, who presumably follow Chinese customs, Yi, or will they henceforth be counted among the Zhuxia 諸夏 ("the many Xia")? Is anyone keeping track? Efforts to classify the population of China have taken many forms over history, often a racial or genealogical form, but for now let the problem be framed in terms of culture or indeed of poetics. Do the authors of the "Bailang Songs" speak from an alien point of view, or do they speak from a point of view so closely identified with that of the Chinese empire that it might as well be Chinese? The ability to make such fine distinctions falls into the cracks between the Bailang text of the songs and their Chinese translation. For although we have what purports to be the words of the songs in the Bailang language, transcribed into Eastern Han Chinese, we do not have a reliable lexicon or grammar of Bailang. The fact that the Chinese text as given in the *Hou Han shu* is so neatly composed in regular four-character verses with end rhymes and adorned with allusions to the *Book of Songs* and the *Analects* leaves us room to wonder how much in the comprehensible text is a free elaboration by the translating officials of some original that might have had quite a different style and content. Once again, this seems to be translation as citation, a translation that anticipates the needs of the target-language public to such a degree that the source language and its public are lost sight of. Perhaps the accompanying officials wrote in Chinese verse what they thought the Bailang elders ought to have said, or would have said had they had the proper cultural equipment. Yes, the barbarians can sing, but on the condition that their song match Huaxia cultural requirements. Otherwise, their song will have to remain "outside the gate."[26]

Attempting to write up a multicultural history of Chinese literature means dashing the two words "multicultural" and "literature" against each other. The very concept of literature in East Asia has so persistently been identified with Chineseness, with the models of antiquity, that it has the effect of filtering the corpus of literary texts. Is *wen* 文 an inherently ethnocentric term? Or (if it makes a difference here) a culturocentric one? Remember Dao'an and the *Baihutong* authors: the former points out that Indian Buddhist texts prize "matter" or "substance" and Chinese audiences love "pattern" 二者胡經尚質，秦人好文. The latter state baldly that "the Yi and Di are to be identified with matter, they are not as capable of refinement as the people of the Central States" 夷狄質，不如中國文. A system of correlations seems to develop here, where Chineseness and *wen* occupy a central position, and a rotating cast of Others, who supply *zhi* but no *wen*, matter but no pattern, fill out the rest of the world. One recognizes the echo of Confucius in the *Analects*, pointing out the deficiency of an overabundance of *zhi*, which makes for savagery, as opposed to an overabundance of *wen*, which makes for pedantry.[27] The difficulty of people from outside the culture of the Central States ever reaching the status of *wen* or participating in the creation of the kind of texts we have come to regard as the literary inheritance of China takes many forms: sometimes outright exclusion, sometimes transformation in the course of appropriation, sometimes what I call evaporation, where a foreign cultural product subsists only as a name, a vestige, or a tune.

After the collapse of the Han, many dynasties and would-be dynasties ruled over parts of China. Quite a few of these were, technically speaking, "barbarian": lineages that had originated among the Xianbei 鮮卑, the Tuoba 拓拔, or other groups ruled over a territory with an administration patterned on that of the Han, with ideologies of rulership that mixed the Zhou classics with the traditions of the steppe and Buddhist political theory. The ruling families of the Northern Wei, the Liao, the Jin, and even the great Tang were of foreign or mixed origin.[28] One of the most capable Chinese emperors, Taizong of the Tang, whose Turkic affiliations were no secret, rebutted in these words an official who was urging him to strike hard and eliminate the foreigners in the empire's midst:

夷狄亦人耳，其情與中夏不殊。人主患德澤不加，不必猜忌異類。蓋德澤洽，則四夷可使如一家；猜忌多，則骨肉不免為讎敵。[29]

The Yi and Di are human beings too, and their feelings are not much different from those of the Chinese. The lord of men is anxious only about failing to benefit others; there is no need to be suspicious of people of a different kind. Through benevolence, the Four Barbarians can be made to join us in a single family, but if suspicion predominates, we cannot even be sure our own flesh and bone is on our side.

With such examples in mind, it became harder to deny the Yi a role in the shaping of Chinese civilization. The high literary culture changed more slowly, however. To write was to adopt the enduring, resistant forms handed down from the past. After the Six Dynasties, the Sui, and the Tang, multicultural China was a reality, and the insistence on archaism, on returning to the fundamentals, on the purity of the Classics, sounds very much like a refusal to recognize what was actually going on and to substitute standards for observations.[30]

Barbarian song survives in ethnographic writing: for example, the memoirs on foreign nations that fill up the last few chapters of each dynastic history (even when the ruling family of the dynasty was itself of foreign origin), or biographies of individuals who deal with the aliens or turn out to have a hybrid past. In the year 546, while besieging the Western Wei stronghold of Yubi, the general Gao Huan 高歡, whose son went on to found the Northern Qi dynasty, fell ill from shock at the loss of much of his army. In a bid to weaken the attackers' will, the defenders claimed that Gao Huan had died. Forcing himself up from his sickbed, Gao asked the Xianbei general Hulü Jin 斛律金 to strike up a song from their common birthplace of Chi-le and sing along with him. It goes:

敕勒川，陰山下。天似穹廬，籠蓋四野。
天蒼蒼，野茫茫。風吹草低見牛羊。[31]

The Chi-le River flows beneath Mount Yin.
The heavens are like a yurt cover
Thrown over the four directions.
The heaven, so vast,
The wilds, so infinite—
The wind blows, the grass parts, cattle and sheep appear.

The *Yuefu shiji* adds: "This song was originally in the Xianbei language. It has been translated into Qi words, and for that reason its lines are of unequal length." No Xianbei original has been preserved, and the text can be traced back no farther than the Northern Song. According to a modern literary historian, this composition "depicts the landscape of the wide prairie in the north and the nomadic life. . . . The boundless and eternal infinity of the scene also reflects the broad mind and heroic spirit of the singer."[32] That's what you would expect from a nomadic steppe dweller, isn't it? Not refinement but a naïve depiction of the reality of the steppes, with an authorial personality to suit. Here indeed barbarians may sing, and not necessarily a song of their submission to imperial norms; but the alternative to the style of the Bailang elders is simply a song about being a nomad, wild and free in an immense natural landscape. If you should seek information about the Chi-le and their song in dictionaries or on Wikipedia, here is what you get:

我國古代北方少數民族之一，以游牧為生。[33]

One of our country's northern national minorities in ancient times. They lived from nomadic pasturage.

敕勒歌的誕生時代，正是我國歷史上南北朝時的北朝時期。此時，今黄河流域以北基本在我國少數遊牧民族鮮卑族的統治之下。敕勒，在漢代時稱屬丁零，魏晉南北朝時稱狄歷、敕勒，到隋朝時稱作鐵勒。[34]

The origins of the "Chi-le Song" date to the Northern Dynasty period in the Northern and Southern Dynasties era of our country's history. At that time, the area north of today's Yellow River basin was for the most part ruled by the Xianbei, one of the nomadic-pastoral national minorities of our country. The Chi-le were known as the Dingling in the Han Dynasty; in the Wei-Jin Southern-and-Northern Dynasties period they were known as the Dili and Chi-le; and starting in the Sui Dynasty they were known as the Tiele.

These descriptions reflect current mainland policy on the teaching of Chinese history, but they are absurdly anachronistic. In the Northern and Southern Dynasties, the Chi-le were hardly "one of our national minorities, living from nomadic pasturage," but a leading military and political force; had they been in charge of writing the entries for prospective twenty-first-century historical dictionaries, they might well have described the Huaxia as "one of our national minorities, who live from grain cultivation and weaving." Rather too obviously in this case, history, lexicography even, is written by the winners long after the battle is done. But in the moment of the song's composition, the future was wide open, though it may take some imagination on our part to recover it. To do so is a form of resistance required of us, lest we fall into the habit that James Scott calls "seeing like a state."[35] (You know which state I mean; it's the one that decides who is a "national minority" and who is not; I don't think we have to worry about seeing like the long-gone Chi-le state.) Let us imagine a Chi-le perspective, insofar as we can, on the singing of the song. Gao Huan, a Xianbei-ized Han general, ill, dejected, and rumored to be dead, calls his companion-in-arms Hulü Jin to remind him and their soldiers, in a song, of what they have in common, their Xianbei background, symbolized by the vast landscape and mobile riches that make the Chi-le invincible in the long term. Maybe he is thinking of making a run for it and retiring to those peaceful pasturelands. In any case, Hulü Jin's singing is an ethnic performance meant to make an impression on a mixed audience of Xianbei and Han hearers, and in no way an accommodation to Han norms (despite the fact that it survives only in Chinese translation; and even then the anthologist almost apologizes for its irregularity—having been "translated into Qi words . . . its lines are of unequal length"). In the end the song has the desired effect of encouraging the troops (and perhaps reminding them of Hulü Jin's loyalty to Gao Huan?), and the battle is won. The victorious Gao Huan eventually makes his son the first emperor of the Eastern Wei dynasty.

A Tuyuhun song, mentioned and preserved only in Chinese translation, comes with an origin story recorded in the *Jin shu*.

> 吐谷渾，慕容廆之庶長兄也，其父涉歸分部落一千七百家以隸之。及涉歸卒，廆嗣位，而二部馬鬥，廆怒曰：「先公分建有別，奈何不相遠離，而令馬鬥！」吐谷渾曰：「馬爲畜耳，鬥其常性，何怒於人！乖別甚易，當去汝於萬里之外矣。」於是遂行。廆悔之，遣其長史史那樓馮及父時耆舊追還之。吐谷渾曰：「先公稱卜筮之言，當有二子克昌，祚流後裔。我卑庶也、理無並大，今因馬而別，殆天所啟乎！諸君試驅馬令東，馬若還東，我當相隨去矣。」樓馮遣從者二千騎，擁馬東出數百步，輒悲鳴西走。如是者十餘輩，樓馮跪而言曰：「此非人事也。」遂止。鮮卑謂兄爲阿干，廆追思之，作《阿干之歌》，歲暮窮思，常歌之。

Tuyuhun was the elder half-brother (by a secondary wife) of Murong Wei. Their father, Shegui, had allotted 1,700 families of their tribe to him as serfs. When Shegui died, Murong Wei inherited the chieftainship. When horses from the two halves of the tribe fought, Wei said angrily: "Our late father divided our people so as to keep them separate, so how is it that we are not keeping apart, but our horses are fighting among themselves!" Tuyuhun said: "Horses are merely livestock. Fighting is in their nature. Why make this into a quarrel among people? But it's easy to leave: I will put ten thousand leagues between you and me." Then he departed. Wei regretted the incident and sent his father's chief counselor, Shina Loufeng, along with other elders from his father's day in pursuit to bring him back. Tuyuhun said: "Our late father had a prognostication to the effect that 'he would have two sons of great ability who would confer blessings on their descendants.' But as I am of inferior birth, we cannot be equally great. If now we separate on account of fighting horses, might this not be a confirmation of Heaven's design? Gentlemen, try turning my horses back toward the east. If they return east, I will follow them too." Loufeng and his twelve hundred mounted men compelled the horses to go a few hundred paces eastward, but the horses constantly moaned and ran back westward. This happened ten or more times. Finally Loufeng knelt down and spoke: "It is not the doing of men." So he gave up. The Xianbei call elder brothers "Agan." Thinking back on his elder brother, Wei composed the "Song of Agan." At the waning of the year, turning the episode over in his mind, he sang it again and again.

Conflict between the brothers is avoided by letting them both be leaders, but of separate peoples. However, there is regret on both sides. The song addressed by Murong Wei to his brother Tuyuhun runs:

阿干西，我心悲，
阿干欲歸馬不歸。
為我謂馬何太苦？
我阿干為阿干西。
阿干身苦寒，
辭我大棘住白蘭。
我見落日不見阿干，
嗟嗟！
人生能有幾阿干。[36]

Agan has left for the west, I am downhearted,
Agan wanted to come back, but the horses would not
    come back.

Ask the horses for me, must there be such suffering?
Our Agan has gone off to the west.
Agan endures bitter cold,
He left us for the desert where the Bailang dwell.
We see the setting sun but no longer see Agan,
Alas!
When will I ever meet another Agan?

This is apparently that rare thing—a poem from the "barbar-ians" that is not about their relation to the Chinese. It comes with an origin story that is also the origin story of two mighty peoples. It marks the separation of the Murong and Tuyuhun clans, who will go on to figure largely in Asian history, and situates the mo-ment of poetic composition in a political crisis, as the prefaces of the *Book of Songs* often do. With these historical functions in mind, I would consider the poem, even apart from its status as a transla-tion, a hybrid text combining some features of the steppe song with some features of Chinese classical composition. Also symp-tomatic of its uncertain place among works of literature for people of the premodern era is the fact that the *Jin shu* gives the circum-stances of its composition and the title but no song; for that you have to go to much later compilations. The *Yuefu shiji*, for example, lists a number of similar titles among the "hengchui ge" 橫吹歌 (flute songs) with a nomad or frontier background but does not contain this lyric. Indeed, the earliest printing of the "Song of Agan" that I have been able to find so far is in a local gazetteer for Gaolan County, compiled in 1775.[37] So several alternatives offer themselves to us. It is possible, but hard to prove, that oral trans-mission carried the song through fifteen hundred years of history and translation into Chinese; it is more likely, I think, that the "Song" as we have it today is a later reconstruction reflecting what someone thinks Murong Wei ought to have said rather than what he said. This does not in the least hinder scholars who quote, an-thologize, and interpret the "Song of Agan" from citing in their footnotes the *Jin shu* as if that historical work were the source for the poem rather than just the source of the story about the poem's creation. It is as if no one wanted to admit that the song is really a piece of synthetic folklore. As with the "Chi-le ge," the text attests to the belief that the barbarians do sing, because we know what they should have sung and the circumstance is too important to let it pass without a song.

I have by no means exhausted the stock of translated foreign poetry in pre-nineteenth-century Chinese, though the archive is not a huge one. The conditions leading to the patchy survival of foreign song texts in premodern China include the restrictive literary codes I've mentioned; a lack of translators; the passage of time; the sheer variety of idioms that had contributed to the musical repertoire; and the fact that the words were often noted just as a means of recording the tune, which itself often eventually faded from memory. I should not like to give the impression that premodern Chinese people were uniquely chauvinistic. The Greeks and Romans were hardly any better at preserving or appreciating the traces of alien creativity. Julius Caesar led a massive expedition into Gaul and wrote a short ethnography of its inhabitants; in it you will find no summaries of their literature, no vocabulary lists, only personal and place-names of the kind that you also find copiously recorded in the Chinese dynastic histories.[38] A major civilization often obliterates those around it. Against this tendency, the collecting habits of Chinese courts, which, despite all the exclusionary theories of Confucian ideologues, continued to treasure tunes and rhythms from outside the realm, are a cultural recognition of the hybridity that was the lived reality of Chinese people in all ages. Massive importation of foreign music occurred under every imperial dynasty. The *Dynastic Histories* enumerate the troops of musicians imported, like tribute, from the kingdoms of Korea, from India, from Central Asia, and other borderlands; they catalog the titles of imported musical works as well. But the people charged with preserving this music were often careless: though the song titles might survive, the words of foreign songs were evanescent. As we read in the *Jiu Tang shu* (Old history of the Tang),

《北狄樂》，其可知者鮮卑、吐谷渾、部落稽三國，皆馬上樂也。... 今存者五十三章，其名目可解者六章；《慕容可汗》、《吐谷渾》、《部落稽》、《鉅鹿公主》、《白淨皇太子》、《企喻》也。其不可解者，咸多「可汗」之辭。... 北虜之俗，呼主為可汗。吐谷渾又慕容別種，知此歌是燕、魏之際鮮卑歌。歌辭虜音，竟不可曉。... 雖譯者亦不能通知其辭，蓋年歲久遠，失其真矣。[39]

What is known as "the music of the Northern Yi" includes that of the Xianbei, the Tuyuhun, and the Buluoji. This is all horseback music [i.e., northern songs with flute and drum accompaniment]. . . . Fifty-three compositions of this kind subsist today, and six titles can still be understood: "The Khan of the Murong Clan," "Tuyuhun," "Buluoji," "The Princess of Julu," "The Suddhodana Prince," and "Qiyu." The songs that cannot be understood contain many repetitions of the word "Khan." The northern savages call their leader "Khan." The Tuyuhun are an offshoot lineage of the Murong, and it appears that the song bearing their name arose as a Xianbei song on the border of Yan and Wei. The song's words are nomad sounds and cannot be understood. . . . Not even the translators are able to understand all the words. It is most likely that the song's authentic wording has been lost to the passage of time anyway.

The border is everywhere in Tang poetry, and not just as a marker denoting the outside of China. In literary contexts, however, it often subsists only as a shell of former meanings. The disappearance of foreign content, leaving only titles and tunes, is visible throughout Guo Maoqian's vast collection *Yuefu shiji* (A compendium of "Music Bureau" poems, ca. 1090). The music and poetry of the Tang court were full of importations; the Dunhuang caves show tremendous intellectual and artistic traffic with other realms among commoners, traders, monks, and performers—something we could not know without the preserved records of that outpost.[40] But if we were to trust the conventional literary histories of China, such contributions were only marginal and superficial, not affecting the consistent stream of development from the *Shijing* onward. The more we familiarize ourselves with the lived multiculturalism of Chinese history, the more we learn to distrust literary history, which comes to appear to be a device for asserting identity despite change.[41]

3

The *Hanzi wenhua quan*: Center, Periphery, and the Shaggy Borderlands

「漢字文化圈」：中心、邊陲與荒野

ARGUING FOR THE IMPORTANCE of translation as a literary dynamic in Chinese literature, and East Asian literature more broadly, I run immediately into some significant objections by intelligent, well-read people. Joseph Allen expresses skepticism about the utility of translation studies in the Asian domain, contending that "translation studies, in all its forms, is European because the problematic of translation is a non-Asian (or at least a non–East Asian) construction."[1] Chinese discourse on translation is unjustifiably promoted, in his view, by recent scholarship. There is no need to construct out of old documents a theory of translation, let alone "our own [Chinese] systematic theory of translation" 我國自成體系的翻譯理論, as Luo Xinzhang puts it.[2] "Of course," Allen concedes,

translation (or interpretation) existed in the ancient Chinese world as did other forms of cultural intercourse, yet, judging from the historical record, which is naturally elite and canonical, there was little intellectual stake in those translational moments. . . . Translation was an instrument of critical change but not an object of critical attention. This is an early and nearly complete form of the invisibility of translation, an invisibility brought on not by hegemonic blindness but by an inherent lack of interest. (122, 135)

The successful promulgation of Chinese script in Korea and Japan "conflated the foreign and the domestic into one undelineated linguistic territory" (131). Translation was unthinkable over this territory because there was, in short, nothing to translate. Now if translation is unimportant, a number of concepts can also be removed from center stage: "the incommensurate nature of languages, the problematic of untranslatability, the tension created by a plurality of languages and their 'nations'" (120). Allen's conclusion coincides in some ways with Liang Qichao's judgment in 1920: "In ancient times our nation was often in contact with alien races. But the foreigners' culture was always treated as lower than our own, and the relationship was always conducted using our language and characters. The dragoman was not worth mentioning" 我國古代與異族之接觸雖多，其文化皆出我下，凡交際皆以我族語言文字 為主，故"象鞮"之業，無足稱焉.[3] But Liang was diagnosing a bias in the culture, and Allen is locating bias in the objections to the bias.[4] The fact that "elite and canonical" sources disregard a thing does not mean that that thing is unimportant. I do not see how Allen can so easily disavow what he calls, with a Gramscian flourish, "hegemonic blindness."

Wiebke Denecke similarly contends that the modern-day concept of translation is blinkered by ethnocentric prejudice. Premodern East Asia, in her view, did quite well without translation. "The Chinese script," as she puts it, "explored dimensions of literary expression closed to alphabetic scripts and . . . enabled a multilingual East Asian 'world without translation,' unifying . . . dialects or languages that were mutually unintelligible in speech, but identical in writing."[5] Her case is based largely on the Japanese practice of *kundoku* or glossing of Chinese written texts, but the model would hold equally well for Korean or Vietnamese or indeed for different vernacular languages spoken within China (what are conventionally called dialects). "*Kundoku* is not translation in any conventional sense, because there is only one text (not an original and a translation). Also, most Japanese practitioners of *kundoku* were monolingual and did not conceive of Chinese texts as texts in a foreign language. Learning *kundoku* did not involve learning a foreign language, it simply required a certain kind of literacy training" (210–11). Yukino Semizu calls this glossing practice "invisible translation," but for Denecke that description does not go far enough.[6] "Translation is indispensable only with phonetic scripts."[7] If we take a logographic script as the norm, we see that phonetic writing has the very great disadvantage of making foreign texts impenetrable to those who do not speak their language. "Educated elites in traditional East Asia," on the contrary, "had direct access to Chinese texts (and audiences) without the need for translation." Furthermore, she charges, "the hegemony of the alphabet is an artifact of colonialism, ultimately going back to the Hellenistic and Roman empires and to the particular success of their heirs in the early modern period in spreading their script to the entire globe" (214).

I think it is not too late to congratulate Chinese authors and script architects, too, for creating a space of *tongwen* 同文 and a degree of success in making their characters understood across a good part of the globe. But the "Chinese cultural sphere" (including the old zones of settlement and migration as well as jet-age diasporas) is today a zone of interestingly contested identities. Nowhere is it more so than in Taiwan, where the question of how much the locally received ways of living and thinking owe to China implies broad social consequences: Is Taiwan after all a province of China, a colonial dependency, or an offshoot, and does anyone have the will, the ability, or the desire to talk back to the "Chinese cultural sphere" rather than speaking only within it and according to its rules? In what would such a "talking back" consist anyway?[8] If we want to think about East Asia as a region replete with former colonial territories, some of which have experienced eras of domination by different powers and indeed periods of self-determination, but above all as a region where the statuses of "colony" and "nation" are not fated or permanent, we will want to ask about the intertwining of script, communication technologies, and political influence. What are the cultural and political implications of the invention of Korean *han'gul*, Japanese *hiragana* and *katakana,* or the various Vietnamese writing systems including present-day romanization? Those writing systems inherit features of the Chinese character, have long interacted with the Chinese character, but are not fully interoperable with it: the tendency over time is to diverge, first in a diglossia and sometimes eventually in a monoglossia (North Korea's rejection of Chinese characters representing an extreme case). Kornicki and Handel document the varieties of vernacularization in and around China, Kornicki with more attention to historical process and Handel with more attention to functional description.[9] When Chinese script traveled, it did not impose a standard pronunciation on its readers; foreigners read the signs out in their own languages. The vocalization of a Chinese text could become an object of reading in its own right; that is, it might be captured in script (e.g., in *hiragana*) and transmitted from one reader to another. Selected Chinese characters, used not for their meanings but for their sound-values, might be mapped onto the sounds of the receiving language, as we have seen being done with the songs in the Yue and Bailang languages; other, nonphonetic marks might be added to provide grammatical guidance in interpretation; eventually a new writing system might develop out of these supplementary marks that "accompanied" (as in the Japanese term *okurigana* 送り仮名) the original signs.[10] Or in other places where Chinese script coexisted with other scripts, educated vernacular readers developed strategies of substitution for mirroring the meaning of Chinese texts with the sounds and written marks of their own language. When Tang- or Song-dynasty Uyghurs read texts in classical Chinese, they might perform a phonetic adaptation of the Chinese words to their local speech, or else substitute the words of the original with semantically equivalent words and terms in Uyghur.[11] Similar techniques are recorded for Khitan and Jurchen readers. The Xixia/Tanguts developed their own writing, logographic and not phonetic, in emulation of the Chinese script and translated a large part of the Chinese literary heritage, so that "an educated Tangut individual would have been fully versed in Chinese literary culture and yet potentially not understand a word of [spoken or written] Chinese."[12] As Tibetans, Mongolians, Uyghurs, and Manchus had previously become acquainted with scripts unrelated to Chinese, perhaps the idea that a single character stood for a single concept was not persuasive to them; they more readily turned Chinese texts into texts readable in their own scripts through paraphrase and rewriting. For them the model whereby the local reader merely performed a vocalization of Chinese script was only one option, and not necessarily the favored one.

Moreover, it is a distortion to think of Chinese script as necessarily functioning in a logographic way, in contrast to other, phonetic, scripts. The oldest surviving versions of the *Yuanchao mishi* 元朝秘史 (Private history of the Yuan dynasty; better known as *Secret History of the Mongols*; in Mongolian, *Mongqol-un niuča to[b] ča'an*) use Chinese characters to represent the sounds of the Mongolian language, much as the transcribers of the *Kojiki* and other early Japanese books had done. This is not to say that the work was created in and for Chinese characters; the linguistic texture of the North and Northwest is far too complex for that. The *Secret History* was apparently first notated in the Uyghur phonetic script, as adapted to Mongolian, but no copy of this original survives. Chinese editions of the work, first printed in 1403–1405, supply two parallel columns, both in Chinese characters, but one giving the Mongolian sound transcription and the other giving a semantic gloss in literary Chinese. "CHENGJISI. A name. HEHANNA. Emperor's. HUZHAWUER. Root origins."—so reads the first line, with glosses, of the bilingual text: "Origins of the Emperor Genghis Khan."[13] The manuscript of the Mongolian text transcribed

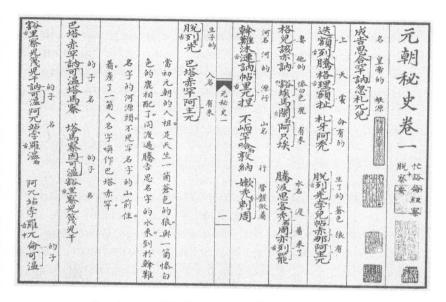

Opening page of the *Yuanchao mishi* (*Sibu congkan* edition, Shanghai: Shangwu, 1936), 1/1a-b.

into Chinese characters was "mined" for examples to furnish a manual of the Mongolian language published in 1389 under the title *Huayi yiyu* 華夷譯語 (A Sino-foreign translation vocabulary)[14]— for the Mongols' Ming successors were acutely aware of the need to train intermediaries in foreign languages and customs. A free translation into Chinese was also produced for the use of historians who were not skilled in Mongolian.[15] Produced by Mongolians and Chinese working together, the bilingual *Yuanchao mishi* is obviously a translation between languages. And that should not surprise us. The Mongol world, briefly stretching from Korea to Poland and southward to Vietnam, was certainly not a "world without translation."

As this wider set of relationships between Chinese texts and foreign publics comes into view, we see that the "Chinese-character sphere" or *hanzi wenhua quan* 漢字文化圈 has many different kinds of borders, internal and external. One kind of border is semantic. Within China, one stumbles on nonsense words and names, relics of lost languages that have been preserved in Chinese-character transcription. The *Huainanzi* 淮南子 mentions place-names with inauspicious connotations: "Zengzi extolled the principle of filial piety, and so he refused to enter the village of Shengmu, 'Defeating Mothers'; Mozi despised music, and so he would not enter the town of Zhaoge, 'Dawn Song.'" 曾子立孝，不過勝母之間；墨子非樂，不入朝歌之邑.[16] Repeated by Liu Xiang 劉向 in *Shuo yuan* 説苑 and *Xin xu* 新序, this example of ritual avoidance was sufficiently well known to be used in a petition by Zou Yang 鄒陽 recorded in the *Shiji*: "There is a county named Shengmu, 'Defeating Mothers,' and Confucius's disciple Zengzi refused to enter it. There is a town named Zhaoge, 'Dawn Song,' and Mozi turned his carriage back rather than pass through it" 縣名勝母而曾子不入，邑號朝歌而墨子回車.[17] Wang Chong 王充 reacted with characteristic skepticism: for him, these place-names were meaningless deposits of chance and the passage of time, and the scruples of those ancient worthies were unjustified. "If there is a village called Shengmu, shall we say that there was really a son who defeated his mother? If a town is called Zhaoge, shall we say that its inhabitants rise up in the morning and sing?" 里名勝母，可謂實有子勝其母乎？邑名朝歌，可謂民朝起者歌乎？[18]

Those place-names doubtless perpetuate words in extinct languages formerly current in Lu and Wei, and if they challenge interpretation, their absurdity is a kind of border separating the past from present understanding. Defeating mothers and singing in bed would be evidence of cultural difference, to be sure, and the moral programs of Zengzi and Mozi would certainly try to suppress such customs; but Wang Chong's suspicion that custom and meaning are not in the least involved is more archaeological in spirit. Place-names are palimpsests. They imperfectly overwrite the traces of the past. Something remains to remind us that the graphs and meanings of standard Chinese have not always covered the map. Nor do they cover the whole of the map. When Fang Xiaobiao and his family were forced to take the road to

Manchurian exile in 1659, one sign of their alienation was the gradual encroachment of incomprehensible place-names like "Ningguta," "Aji," and "Liaoshen bila."[19]

Another kind of border is graphic. If the transition, mediated by writing, from China to the daughter cultures of Korea, Japan, and Vietnam is apparently smooth (though not borderless), the transition to the cultures of the Northwest, West, and Southwest is rough and shaggy. Attempting to describe the Chinese script's sphere of influence through a negation of alphabetic writing, as a "world without translation," simplifies by excluding both a great deal of cultural variability and the many historical processes and practices through which reading methods come to be. The proclamation of an alternative world of communication without phonetic signs begins to look, once more, like the abrupt and authoritative act whereby the sage-emperor creates commonality: "Today across the realm cart-tracks are of one size and writing is done with the same characters" 今天下車同軌，書同文.[20] *Kundoku* 訓讀, that reading "without translation," as Denecke would have it, or in "invisible translation," as Semizu would have it, is possible only after readers have acquired competence in the Chinese character. Did they reach that competence without reliance on sound? That seems improbably austere. Reading tended to be phonetic—to judge from the documentation supplied by Kornicki and Galambos, people apparently felt that to decode a passage of writing, it was necessary to voice the characters somehow—although the particular pronunciation used by the authors of a Chinese text was without consequences for the text's currency. Few people traveled between Japan and China, so pronunciation standards tended to be set locally, sometimes on a historical basis, sometimes on a semantic one. The reader and his or her immediate culture decided. "Texts produced in the cosmopolitan written form . . . were performed and consumed in the vernacular."[21]

Now was this vernacularization a translation or not? Was it a passage into another language or an extension of the Chinese language to a new geographical and phonetic area? Kornicki sees things differently from Denecke. "Vernacular reading," according to him, "is nothing more than a process or procedure applied to a text. What comes out of this procedure (whether orally, silently, or in writing), on the other hand, is indubitably a translation. It is, however, what I am going to term a 'bound translation.' . . . The 'bound translation' allowed you to read it (aloud) but provided no explanation of the sense: the reader either had to have expert sinological knowledge or to consult other commentaries and exegetical works."[22] Precisely: vernacular reading was not intended to supply new content; for the content, the reader had to depend on his or her knowledge of other Chinese texts. It might be that the Japanese or Korean public had internalized the meanings of Chinese characters and passages to such a degree that they no longer seemed to be "foreign" (after all, we are talking about cultural relations developed over a millennium or two). No meanings were supposed to be generated in the territory of arrival—at least, as long as reading Chinese was felt to be a borderless merging with a universal civilization. But with the passage of time, as rival centers of authority emerged and the erstwhile peripheral peoples claimed space for critique and debate, vernacular reading began to look more and more like translation. Ogyū Sorai (荻生徂徠, 1666–1728), for example, insisted that Chinese was "an alien language and had to be dealt with on its own terms."[23] Habitual equivalences between Chinese terms and Japanese terms were to be questioned. "What was driving his arguments was his conviction that Zhu Xi and other thinkers of the Song dynasty had misunderstood and overinterpreted the classics."[24] It was important, therefore, for Ogyū to be able to say that a reading was not simply the local phonetic clothing of a timeless, universal idea but an interpretation, an opinion, and thus something that might be displaced by a better opinion. Similarly, in Korea "some scholars were very uneasy about the idea of establishing a set of official translations for the Chinese classics and printing them, for that would fix the interpretation of those texts for good, and it would leave scholars little room for debating" them (200–201). "Vernacular reading," says Kornicki, "surely worked: it gave you access to any Sinitic text, ancient or modern, and it subverted the 'Chineseness' of texts by making them linguistically and aurally familiar" (185). But when it became too natural, too familiar, to be questioned, it also subverted the peripheral reader's ability to decide what the meaning of the text was to be.

In a purely descriptive sense, too, if communication with foreigners were to happen entirely without translation, if univocal meanings were definitely established, then some of the ambiguities and exploitation of ambiguities that surely happened in history must be ruled out. Whether something is a translation or not, whether a language is foreign or not, depends on what you are trying to do, what you are trying to prove. The dissident scholars just mentioned appealed to the foreignness of Chinese texts in order to unsettle the sedimented meanings they had acquired. Atsuko Ueda finds that "the emergence of [a Japanese] national language in fact appropriated the linguistic space established by *kanbun kundokutai.*"[25] For that to happen, the Chinese meanings associated with Chinese-derived script had first to be treated as occurring in another language, separately from their spoken realization by Japanese readers. The consciousness of one's own language being a different language from the text establishes a distance propitious to critique.

Yet a third kind of border is rhetorical or intentional. According to O. W. Wolters, who may or may not have a revisionist axe to grind, the literate elite of premodern Vietnam "did not actually believe the Chinese classics. Instead . . . [they] cited the Confucian canon only 'to lend weight to specific Vietnamese statements about themselves.' . . . 'fragmenting and detaching passages' and 'detaching those passages of their original textual meaning.'"[26] This complicates, if it does not actually contradict, the notion of a "world without translation." In such cases, the word meanings are not the problem; it is the meaning of the utterance as a whole that is warped or reversed by the person citing it. The very possibility of such a thing happening, it seems to me, requires those

Vietnamese readers and writers to hold Chinese texts at a certain remove, to refuse to accept their utterances as definitively and authoritatively describing this or that situation occurring in Vietnam. To achieve effects that might be described as irony, appropriation, *détournement,* or abuse, they had to be able to handle words provisionally, even cynically, and not assume that their meanings had been settled once and for all. The *hanzi wenhua quan* must have been a loose enough linguistic system to allow for that to happen. Do we call that possibility of difference "translation," "rhetoric," or "pragmatics"? Translation is certainly one name for the opening of a gap between what is said and what is meant, and without some such gap there is no rhetoric, no subjectivity, and no real dialogue.

We have seen that the model of *kundoku* as nontranslation, as pure semantic reading, does not really apply to all the variants of vernacular reception of Chinese texts in the regions of and around China. Perhaps the "world without translation" is really a fantasy of centralization, of identity without difference. If that is so, then Denecke's liberation from the Greco-Roman world comes at a high price—higher, at any rate, than the Vietnamese, according to Wolters, were willing to pay. I would prefer to follow Dagmar Schäfer's recommendation that "sophisticated regional histories of languages enrich historical understandings of translation practices and ways of coping with a multilingual world. . . . We can infer from such examples an expanded understanding of language interaction and that actors made significant methodological choices when they 'translated.'"[27]

Schäfer's use of terms such as "actors" and "choice" reminds us that translation is always undertaken for some reason, to achieve some aim, and the reasons and aims can differ greatly among cases of translation. What a technology makes possible and what it is actually used to do may not be the same thing. Kornicki, again: "Translation in pre-modern East Asia was mostly anonymous and mostly one-way. No vernacular works produced in any East Asian society were translated into Sinitic or vernacular Chinese and introduced to Chinese readers. This reflects, on the one hand, the literary self-sufficiency of China, but it also shows that the language communities of East Asia were on the whole uninterested in cultural exports."[28] Kornicki cites Ch'oe Haenggwi 崔行歸 (908–978) complaining that Chinese do not read poems by Koreans (these would have been poems in Chinese, of course). On the other hand, it was possible, in another story told by Kornicki, for two diplomats, one Korean and one Vietnamese, meeting in Beijing, to exchange poems in literary Chinese, each praising his own homeland as the place where the codes of ritual and music were followed most scrupulously.[29] It is for a moment as if the stage had been yielded to these cultural inheritors, as if China itself had been transcended.

The formula of the *Hanzi wenhua quan*, this zone where translation is not necessary, applies more or less smoothly only to one part of the wider world immediately affected by Chinese culture. It is actually a monocultural model restricted to certain classes of people in certain areas, and mainly a model for the diffusion outward of Chinese ways. Even in Korea, Japan, and Vietnam—the "good students" of Chinese classicism—a great deal of culture, and not only popular culture, took place outside the sphere of Chinese-character communication. We should not ignore the communicative traffic on the borders of China that involves demonstrably foreign languages and writing systems: depending on the era, we might be enumerating the Sogdian and Khitan polities, Manchuria, Mongolia, the Uyghur caliphates, the Tangut empire, Tibet: areas touched by writing systems derived from India (as in Tibet) or from Aramaic (like Old Uyghur, Mongol, and the Manchu script devised in the seventeenth century), not to mention Arabo-Persian. Indeed in large parts of Ming-dynasty China, not to mention the expansions of the Qing, the Chinese written language was a recent arrival.[30] There are also Sinitically derived scripts like Old Zhuang, modern Zhuang, and the "women's writing" of Hunan, none of which are interchangeable with Chinese characters.[31] To take the putative *Hanzi wenhua quan* as the preeminent pattern for the diffusion of Chinese culture is to ignore a large part, indeed the most challenging and therefore most interesting part, of the story of Chinese multiculturalism.

"One-way translation," as Kornicki calls it, describes the diffusion of the most influential texts in Chinese: the Classics, the books studied by administrators and examination candidates, and (once its Chinese translation had been settled) the Buddhist Tripitaka. They flowed out of China and were often promulgated by states eager to educate, that is, Confucianize and Sinicize, their populations. Not much flowed back in the other direction; given "the literary self-sufficiency of China," there was little demand there for works written abroad.

Written culture flowed out of China more readily than it flowed in, but even in the outward direction there could be impediments. If we suppose, as is natural for people living in a globalized commercial society to do, that the ideal was to achieve the widest possible distribution for Chinese cultural products, we will fail to capture the thinking of the officials in charge of international relations. Consider this episode from the shared history of Tibet and China. In the tradition of "marriage diplomacy" (*heqin* 和親), Chinese princesses had on occasion been married to the rulers of Tibet. In the year 730 the Jincheng Princess 金城公主, one such consort, sent a message home to the Tang court requesting copies of the *Shijing*, the *Zuo zhuan*, the *Li ji*, and the *Wenxuan*—fundamental texts for any literate person, such as the princess evidently was. The palace secretariat was about to send the books, but an official named Yu Xiulie 于休烈 quickly sent in a memorial opposing any such thing:

戎之生心, 不可以無備; 典有恒制, 不可以假人。... 昔者東平王入朝, 求《史記》、諸子, 漢帝不與, 蓋以《史記》多兵謀, 諸子雜詭術。夫以東平漢之懿戚, 尚不欲示征戰之書, 今西戎國之寇讎, 豈可貽經典之事? 且臣聞吐蕃之性, 慓悍果決, 敏情特銳, 喜學不回, 若達於書, 必能知戰。深於《詩》, 則知武夫有師幹之試; 深於《禮》, 則知《月令》有廢興之兵; 深於《傳》, 則知用師多詭詐之計; 深於文, 則知往來有書檄之制。何異借寇

兵而資盜糧也？ ... 且公主下嫁從人，遠適異國，合務夷禮，返求
良書，愚臣料之，恐非公主本意也，慮有奔北之類，勸教於
中。若陛下慮失蕃情，以備國信，必不得已，請去《春秋》。當周道既
衰，諸侯強盛，禮樂自出，戰伐交興，情偽於是乎生，變詐
於是乎起，則有以臣召君之事，取威定霸之名。若與此書，國之
患也。[32]

We cannot allow ourselves to fail to anticipate the designs of
the Rong.[33] The Classics contain our permanent institutions
and cannot be lent out to others. . . . Formerly the Prince of
Dongping petitioned to have a personal copy of the *Shiji* 史記
and the philosophical masters, but the Han emperor would not
allow it. The *Shiji* is full of military plans and the philosophers
are full of sophistical arguments. So if even the Prince of Dongping, who was a son of the emperor, was not allowed to possess
books of strategy, in the present case these western barbarians
are marauders and enemies of our State; how is it even imagined
to let them have our Classics? I have heard, concerning the
character of these Tibetans, that they are decisive and sharp-
witted, love to learn and do not fall back once they have made
an advance. If they should acquire our books, they will certainly
use the information in them against us. If they become expert
in the *Book of Poetry* they will learn about the "stalwart defenders" [mentioned in ode 7, "Tu Ju" 兔罝]; if they become expert
in the *Records of Ritual* they will learn our schedule for muster-
ing and dismissing soldiers; if they become expert in the *Zuo
zhuan* they will learn tricks and feints for winning battles; if
they become expert in the *Wen xuan* they will learn to write
dispatches and orders. Why should we offer weapons to rob-
bers and give sustenance to bandits? . . . Now this Princess, having married an inferior, must obey this husband of hers. She is
living among foreigners and is required to follow their outlandish rituals. I suspect that this plan to get useful books [from
China] is not her doing. Rather, some turncoats and deserters
are intervening and directing her. If Your Majesty judges that

making such a gift is necessary in order to maintain good relations with the foreigners and preserve trust in our dynasty, I beg you at any rate to leave out the *Spring and Autumn Chronicles*. The decay of the Zhou institutions, the rise of powerful princes, the anarchy of rites and music, the uninterrupted succession of wars, and the consequent emergence of lying and trickery such that vassals gave orders to sovereigns and rulers vied for the title of hegemon—if you let them have the book containing these things, it will be a disaster for our dynasty.

As we see, in this case not even a fully competent Chinese reader was to be allowed the privilege of reading the Classics from a residence abroad. The problem is not one of translation but of application. Putting the stratagems and precedents of Chinese history in enemy hands would be, in Yu Xiulie's judgment, a huge security leak. And to let foreigners see the *Chunqiu*, that record of a time when good order had decayed, princes made constant war on one another, and deception reigned—if letting outsiders see this immense heap of dirty laundry from the past might bring a loss of national prestige, which is bad enough, in the worst case it is as if letting the Tibetans read the *Spring and Autumn Chronicles* would reanimate the history told in those *Chronicles*. Keeping those crucial books within the borders was a matter of information supremacy. Possessing *wen*, in this account, is not a vague mystical or ethical thing. It is having the books that support a certain way of life.[34] Who should have those books is therefore a sensitive matter. The Jincheng Princess may have possessed *wen* in her individual capacity, but being the wife of an alien, she was in the position of the "barbarized Chinese" raised as a problem by the *Zhou li* commentators and Han Yu. (諸夏有即夷禮者，即夷之也: "Should people of Xia descent perform barbarian rituals, then let them be treated as barbarians."[35]) Thus Yu Xiulie's resistance to book exports. Those books made all the difference between the Hua and the Yi. Yu Xiulie is quick to recognize the inborn ability of the Tibetans. He by no means thinks of them as a lesser breed of humanity: they are quick thinkers and tenacious learners. Though we might imagine that wide circulation confirms cultural prestige, that is not always the case. Here it is rather exclusive possession that demonstrates the power of those cultural goods. The goods are shown to be of a *cultural*, not *ethnic*, nature by the fact that they can be acquired by anybody, Huaxia or not, and that is why the regulator is anxious that they be *politically* restricted.

On several other occasions in Chinese history, the court intervened to forbid the export of canonical books. Under the Han, as Yu Xiulie's memorial recounts, the Prince of Dongping was not permitted to have the *Records of the Grand Historian*, though this was more to do with his bad behavior than with any foreignness. Su Shi argued against letting Koreans and Khitans have Chinese books.[36] On several occasions in the Ming and Qing, foreign missions were forbidden to take books home, particularly maps and geographical works. Something like a technology export license regime surrounded the key works of Chinese culture. On the other hand, Buddhist books were never restricted: religion was not a primary concern of the state, Buddhism was an import anyway, and the dharma teachings were always said to be universal.[37] In the case of the Classics and Histories, language and translation are not the problem at all. It is taken for granted that foreigners can read and understand Chinese. Rather, a social barrier was imposed to make the circulation of information asymmetrical.

Thus the sphere of Chinese-character culture, which might at first glance look like an undivided sea of knowledge exchange, is by no means an intellectual free-trade zone. Differences abound, though "translation" may not quite be the word for the means of negotiating them. This premodern media space is carved up into zones of differential access, prestige, and attention; marked by one-way and two-way flows of information; filtered, layered, and channeled. Charting these flows is *partly* a matter for literary historians, partly a matter of geography, and largely a matter of policy—for this last category defines the kind of document we mainly see: debates about information policy referring to prior ideology. Once cultural diffusion is in play, the terms of the long-consecrated distinction between Hua and Yi are somewhat altered, for the Yi take on some of the characteristics of the Hua and there is a concern that the Hua will become like the Yi in some ways. In debates like that surrounding the Tibetan book export proposal, we can identify three shades of opinion: (a) those who refuse humanity to the aliens; (b) those who think they can be civilized; (c) those who fear they may be civilized. Behind these three options stands a major difference in opinion: whether the Hua/Yi distinction should be strongly or weakly maintained. Those who think there *should be* a strong distinction tend to believe that there already *is* a deep essential difference; those who think there *need not be* such a strong distinction are willing to overlook differences or treat them as merely superficial.

Princess Jincheng's predicament was a familiar one in Chinese poetry: an experience of the borderlands by someone whose strongest ties were with the center. Literary history meets geography on the frontier. The literary frontiers of China are distinct from one another. Each has its modes of writing and sensibility. Let us return briefly to the musical map of China offered in the *Zhou li* and sketched by Yu Siu-wah.

Departing from the center in any direction, we will encounter one of four boundaries. On the east, the Dong Yi: by the Tang dynasty, they are only a name found in old books; their language and ethnic distinctiveness have vanished. Occasionally the old name is reused to label Koreans, Japanese, Okinawans, or other peoples, but once these Yi have accepted the Chinese character as the vehicle of their high culture, communication with them is relatively smooth. Toward the south, the Nan Man are experiencing the push of settlers, armies, refugees, and administrators. Vietnam conserves its Chinese-character heritage, similar to the East. The Tang still saw the South, from Guangxi to Fujian, as remote and exotic.[38] Over the centuries, non-Chinese languages there were largely replaced by Chinese dialects and the speakers of indigenous languages pushed into isolation. Though Han Yu, Liu

Zongyuan, and Su Shi endure exile there, this border zone, like the eastern frontier, does not leave a deep trace in literary writing before the Ming. But the northern and western frontiers, where Chinese contend with nomads, merchants, and rival empires, are zones of intense literary creation. Music, as was indicated in chapter 2, flows across this border and finds a home in Chinese courts and taverns: music from Goguryeo, India, Bukhara, Kucha, Kashgar, Qara-hoja, and the Xianbei and Xiongnu peoples, among others.[39] Poetic genres and topics specific to the North arise. Where the greatest friction between languages and cultures occurs, and where the greatest literary legacy is made out of this friction, is to the north and west, the frontier shared with Xiongnu, Mongol, Manchu, Xianbei, Uyghur, Turkic, Tibetan, Jurchen, Khitan, and other peoples. I am sorry to offer catalogs, but the multiplicity and diversity of the Northwest are inseparable from this literary mode. There are the complaints of women held captive by or bartered in marriage to a northern chieftain, and songs of soldiers sent to guard the northern frontier, marking years and decades of service under the threat of never returning home—to mention just two categories of poem that are extremely well represented in Guo Maoqian's collection of over five thousand *yuefu*. The "Eighteen Songs to a Nomad Flute" ("Hu jia shiba pai" 胡笳十八拍) commemorating Cai Yan 蔡琰 and the legend of Wang Zhaojun 王昭君 are themes spun into endless variations dramatizing the difference between Han and Hu.[40] Tamara Chin characterizes this genre of border lament as starring the "figure of the female Han exile, who remained faithful to her homeland while elaborating a phobic ethnography of the northern nomads."[41] Hundreds of "Sai shang qu" 塞上曲, "Poems Composed on the Mountain Pass," and the like figure in the *Complete Poems of the Tang*. Drinking songs, songs of farewell, songs describing landscape, weather, customs, women, food—but I'm cataloging again. Though these poems certainly reflect encounters with alien peoples, the typical frontier poem is spoken in the voice of a Chinese addressing other Chinese about the frontier. Once in a while it adopts the voice of a non-Chinese, through the kind of fictive vocalization that *yuefu* permitted: "I'm a son of northern barbarians, I don't know any Han songs" 我是虜家兒，不解漢兒歌, says the speaker of one "Zhe yangliu" series, though the point may be to refer to the music, now lost, that was original to the song rather than disclaiming ability to speak the language.[42]

In the North and West, the lands traditionally ascribed to the Di 狄 and Rong 戎, the "Chinese-character cultural sphere" encounters a real Other. This Other either doesn't write at all or writes in an outlandish alphabet. The Others cannot represent themselves (in Chinese); they must therefore be represented.[43] We already saw that when this Other speaks and reads Chinese, the available frames of reference make that linguistic competence a symptom of either submission or subversion (think of the Bailang, on the one hand, and, on the other, of the Tibetans scheming to get their hands on the Chinese Classics). When the foreigner *is* spoken, the ambiguity is resolved, but at the cost of turning the speaker into an object of speech rather than its subject—a situation to which I will turn in more detail in the final chapter, about exile poetry. By incorporating northwestern scenes, people, customs, and situations, the makers of folksongs and the authors of courtly verse were performing a kind of cultural transfer, bringing news from the border regions back to the center. But how? As Cai Yan (or someone impersonating her) says in concluding the "Hu jia shiba pai":

胡笳本自出胡中
緣琴翻出音律同
十八拍兮曲雖終
響有餘兮思無窮

The nomad flute comes from among the Hu.
The green-strung zither translates/transposes its tunes,
     without altering their notes and modes.
Although my song of eighteen verses is now finished,
     its resonance lingers and the thought it expresses will never
     come to an end.

Rescoring the nomadic flute's airs for the metropolitan zither is an act of representation analogous to the transliteration and translation from alien tongues that we have been discussing all along. But is it only an analogy for Cai Yan's act of verse composition?[44] To make the analogy somewhat more persuasive, something more than a mere metaphor, we would need to catalog the tropes, the techniques, the thematic vocabulary of this "frontier-pass literature" (*biansai wenxue* 邊塞文學), describing it, as meticulously as possible, as a distinct language within the wider Chinese poetic language. But how is it made distinct? Imitation of the lyrics that accompanied foreign music doubtless played a role in stimulating the emergence of frontier poetry as a distinct genre; as Timothy Wai Keung Chan has noted, the evocative power of place-names, themselves often clusters of foreign sounds, signals the presence of the frontier in poetry.[45] I do not have room to perform this analysis here; I can only wave in the direction of its desirability (perhaps it calls for statistical investigation and artificial intelligence). But I surmise that the creation of a specific subtype of poetry and the rise in popularity of models for composing it annexed the Northwest to the Chinese poetic universe to such a degree that a poet did not need ever to have trod the soil of that region or encountered any of its natives to turn out effective examples of the genre. The canonical frontier poems of Wang Changling and Li Bai, residents of the capital who (even allowing for Li Bai's exotic persona) never marched along the Wall, demonstrate this autonomy of poetic convention from experience. I take that to be the indication that a language has, to all intents and purposes, taken the place of a purported reality. The Northwest had been translated inward, 譯胡為秦 as Dao'an might say, and become a set of protocols available to any competent poet.

The verbal naturalization of the Northwest through lyric (always the model Chinese literary genre) and through historiography, specifically the "Memoirs on Alien Populations" (四夷志) that are our main source of information on the peoples of the border regions, leads to a place where poetry and history intersect.

Historiography fed the authors of both poems and policy documents by providing material for allusion—anecdotes, examples, names, and places. A Chinese literary imagination of the Northwest framed by history writing and lyric poetry seems almost to point to a space where history would be written as poetry and poems would be received as history, a space that in other cultures is filled by epic. And indeed the modern Chinese term for epic is *shishi* 史詩, "the history poem." But one of the old chestnuts of literary historiography, pulled out and chewed over every generation or two, is that "the Chinese have no national epic."

What does it mean to say that a culture *lacks* something? What if the people living in that culture never felt it as a lack? The Tang dynasty lacked television, for example, but it would be foolish to claim too much significance for that lack. By pointing to the missing epic in China's literary cupboard, Hegel and others (including Hu Shi and Zhu Guangqian) asserted a deficiency, as if every self-respecting culture had to have an epic, and the absence of epics could serve as a diagnosis of some deep flaw in Chinese consciousness.[46] It would be meaningful to say that China lacked an epic only if there was reason to believe that circumstances would have permitted Chinese to have one, or to want one, otherwise. The fact that I lack a television (that's true) tells you something about me, permits you to diagnose me as a snob or an eccentric, only because so many people in our age do have them. You may judge that I am missing out. But if I don't want one, my lack doesn't appear as a lack to me. Has anyone shown that premodern China might, could, or ought to have had epics? Has anyone shown that any Chinese wanted one before the modern era made it seem that epics were essential equipment for developing a national identity?

Though the Chinese literary methods for representing the Northwest—lyric and historiography—can be triangulated to locate where an epic might be found, the actual place of epics is on the other side of the northwestern border. Epic traditions centering on a hero who unites disparate tribes, defeats enemies, and founds a conquering dynasty are the dominant verbal art form over a vast range of territory that is today technically within China but not culturally Chinese. I am forced by the nature of the documentation to talk about recent periods, but it is not unreasonable to suppose that epic composition has been going on for many centuries in Central Asia, Tibet, and the steppes. The Kyrghyz epic of Manas, the Uyghur epic of Oghuz Khan, and the epic of Janggar sung by Mongolians, Kalmyks, and Oirats are all military hero-epics, but the largest share of scholarly attention has gone to the Gesar epic of Tibet. The saga of King Gesar of Ling, which according to its translator Robin Kornman is "generally accepted [as] the longest single piece of literature currently in the world canon, encompassing some 120 volumes and about 20 million words" (not necessarily a recommendation in my view), appears to have arisen in the thirteenth or fourteenth century.[47] It circulates in Mongolian, Manchu, Turkic, Tangut, Ladakh, and other versions, though the Tibetan versions are considered primary. The *Gesar* epic was supported by the institutions of Lamaist Buddhism, the state religion of the Yuan and Qing dynasties, and thus benefited from imperial patronage, however indirect. Printed editions were sponsored in the nineteenth century by learned Lamaist clergy, most notably the influential Jamgön Ju Mipham (1846–1912). It recounts the birth, ordeals, and military campaigns of King Gesar of Ling, who in the epic overcomes adversaries at home, wins a wife, resists the charms of a number of witch-princesses, conquers eighteen strategic castles, and subdues the kingdoms of the Four Quarters to found a realm of peace and justice. Warrior epic, trickster fables, anecdotes of skill, tales of magic, and acts of spiritual combat combine with events from the history of Eastern Tibet in the twelfth century. The non-Tibetan *Gesar*s naturally vary in the episodes included but are recognized as being versions of the same story. Gesar's story shares elements with the other epics mentioned earlier, attesting to a common fund of memory and imagination. The divinified Gesar is honored in temples throughout Tibet, Central Asia, Manchuria, and Mongolia.

In terms of literary geography, the vast and populous land of China, which allegedly lacks an epic, is thus surrounded by epics on three sides. Tibetan, Central Asian, and Mongolian-Manchurian epics are couched in different languages and may celebrate different heroes but otherwise show a remarkable similarity in their themes and performance styles. The epic in full flower was right next door to China, and China was ruled for centuries by peoples who indulged in epic (the Yuan or Mongol dynasty, 1276–1368; the Qing or Manchu dynasty, 1644–1911), but Chinese literati were having none of it. Literary values in China, it seems, implied not a failure to compose epic but an actual rejection of it.

Indeed, acquaintance with epic tradition is a marker of the degree to which the non-Chinese in the later Chinese empire shared cultural resources in which the Chinese took no interest. When the Panchen Lama visited Beijing in 1780, his conversation with the Manchu Qianlong emperor concerned the factual basis of the *Gesar*; the Lama prepared for this interview by gathering information from a learned colleague, the abbot Sumpa Yeshe Paljor.[48] Epic, like Tibetan Buddhism, provided a kind of "cultural glue" for uniting the Inner Asian peoples of the Manchu imperium, but no one ever tried to make it appeal to the Chinese. *Gesar*, the Janggar epic, and the epic of Oghuz Khan were not translated into Chinese until the late twentieth century. The Manchus knew the low regard Chinese had for steppe peoples and nomads (the very people among whom epic has traditionally flourished) and did not seek to spread Manchurian cultural practices among the people they ruled.

The origins of the Gesar, Janggar, and Manas epics are multiple. They arose in a variety of milieus that encouraged cultural mixing: the pan-Asian migrations of Mongol armies, the wanderings of Turkic peoples, the commercial oases of the Silk Road, and the passes between India, Tibet, and Central Asia. One of the formative influences on the *Gesar* epic was the *Ramayana*, available in a condensed Tibetan version from at least the eleventh century. Among the components of the *Gesar* are:

first, the cycle of the Four Sons of Heaven, doubled by the cycle of the *lokapālas* [guardians of the four directions]. . . . For reasons of religious folklore, the representatives of the North, Gesar and Vaisravana, got special emphasis in this cycle. Then came the cycle of [the northern hidden realm] Shambhala and the Ramayana epic. Finally, the epic of the *Tribulations of Pehar*. . . . The *Alexander Romance*, the Sogdian tale of Kysr and the bandits, Indian legends of the *cakravartin* [divine king] and the Wonder-Working Horse, and still others.[49]

This is a characteristically Central Asian mix of "foreign themes transported by Buddhist missionaries, Sogdian merchants, Muslim travelers, obscure marketplace singers and other vagabonds, combined with and superimposed on indigenous Tibetan stories, particularly those from the Amdo region."[50] An oral epic accumulates and digests any material that is seen as valuable for developing its themes. Ironically in light of the history of epics' being claimed as the foundation legends of national uniqueness, oral epics are built from hybrid resources, and Asian nomad epics are particularly so.

A copy of the Mongol text of *Gesar* was printed and stored in the imperial Qing library in 1716. The Chinese label on the outside attests to what seems like a misunderstanding: *Sanguo yanyi* 三國演義, *The Romance of the Three Kingdoms*, it reads.[51] This is a bit like mistaking Goethe's *Faust* for the *Iliad* because Helen of Troy appears in both. Three Tibetan kingdoms do figure in the story, but that does not seem to be the meaning of the title. The title, apparently a misunderstanding, is more probably a bit of crafty cultural policy. One of the heroes of the *Romance of the Three Kingdoms* is Guan Yu 關羽, later deified under the name Guandi 關帝. Temples dedicated to Gesar in the Tibetan, Central Asian, and North Asian areas were known to Chinese-speaking settlers as "temples of Guandi."[52] Anyone who took a good look at the legends, paintings, or statues concerning Gesar would soon understand that here was a different hero, a Buddhist wonder-working warrior king whose efforts at uniting the three Tibetan kingdoms came a thousand years after the division of China into the three kingdoms fought over by Guan Yu and his rivals. However, equating Gesar with Guandi is a comparison just "good enough" to do what it was meant to do, namely, to draw a parallel between heroes of the Chinese and Tibetan communities in a way that served Manchu cultural aims. Since the epic is already such a hybrid, isn't it a continuation of previous practice to invite Guandi to join the parade?

In 2003 the Gesar epic was added to UNESCO's list of items of Intangible Cultural Heritage, and the Chinese government laid out a nine-year action plan for archiving recitations, training young performers, and building performance venues across Tibet, Central Asia, and Inner Mongolia. It may be that by endowing these national minorities' heroic tales with an infrastructure, the modern Chinese state, wrestling with its multicultural and multiethnic makeup, has sought to defuse their autonomist (nation-building) potential. After all, the heroes of the Gesar, Jangghar, Oghuz Khan, and other epics led their armies against rival groups and conquered their neighbors, including, in some instances, China. One report from the *Indian Defence Review* (the standpoint of which should be obvious) views the celebration of the nomadic epic tradition as Machiavellian, suggesting that episodes of the Oghuz Khan epic focusing on Chinese treachery are being revised away and that statements about the relative dating of the Manas and Oghuz Khan epics are to be read not as mere philological disputes, but as an aspect of the contest between Kyrghyz and Uyghurs for cultural preeminence in the region.[53] Present-day China has inherited the boundaries set by the Qing emperors, who established a protectorate over Tibet, conquered the Muslim principalities that now make up Xinjiang, and retained their old base in the steppes of Mongolia and Manchuria. But ruling as a centralized state with a 92 percent Han Chinese majority, China has had to develop cultural policies distinct from the Manchu practice of cultural separateness. Its position on ethnic minorities and national cultural heritage has been developed from the Soviet response to the "nationalities question," with input from professional ethnographers.[54] The official line is that the People's Republic is a *tongyi de duominzu guojia* 同一的多民族國家, a "multiethnic unified nation." This formula allows one to play on the "multiethnic" part or on the "unified" part, depending on the purpose. So now, in his closing speech to the National People's Congress in March 2018, Xi Jinping can claim the *Gesar* and the other epics for "China":

中國人民是具有偉大創造精神的人民。在幾千年歷史長河中 ... 我國產生了老子、孔子、莊子 ... 等聞名于世的偉大思想巨匠 ... 傳承了格薩爾王、瑪納斯斯、江格爾等震撼人心的偉大史詩。[55]

The Chinese people are a people having great creative spirit. In the multimillennial course of history ... our motherland produced Laozi, Confucius, Zhuangzi ... and other world-renowned great masters of thought ... she inherited such soul-shaking great epics as those of King Gesar, Manas, and Janggar.

And indeed the repackaging of these epics as part of *Chinese* cultural inheritance serves political ends, however much it departs from the epics' history, language, and content—and those of Chinese culture too.

In the official Ruist imagination of geography and culture, wild and barbaric peoples are drawn to the Central Regions in search of the civilizing benefits of rites, music, and governance. That cultural goods could come from outside the Chinese domain was unthinkable. Even when China was ruled by "barbarian" dynasties, the realm of culture was, at least in theory, an undiluted heritage of the Chinese sages. Now the Chinese "inheritance" of these epics from the Qing hegemony makes them another venue for the "One Belt One Road" initiative. I do not like to claim that national character never changes, but the repetition of an old scenario strikes me as an instance of cultural inertia.

National claims over cultural property and identity should be a problem, not a solution or an inevitability. Populations, territories, nations, cultures, languages, and communication networks are all independent variables shifting about in space, and literary history should seek to reflect that fact, not suppress it. The next chapter will explore some consequences of such mobility.

4

The Formation of China: Asymmetries in the Writing of History

形塑中國：歷史書寫的若干不對稱性

ETHNICITY HAS OFTEN cropped up in the foregoing chapters, wherever they touched on the differences between *Han* and *Yi*, their place as subjects or objects of representation, or the separations observed, demanded, or enforced between Hua and Yi populations. Many scholars have written about conceptions of race and ethnicity in traditional China, whether to explore semantic categories, to retrace lived experience, or to analyze political and diplomatic discourse.[1] On the broadest scale, historians have sometimes tried to see a pattern in the alternating schools of thought on Hua-Yi relations. For example, Luo Zhitian 羅志田 has claimed that "when Chinese dynasties were strong, they mostly emphasized the open side of the Chinese-barbarian dichotomy, and when the Chinese and barbarians were evenly matched or the barbarians were stronger than the Chinese, the Chinese literati would usually emphasize the negative, closed side. Essentially, [attitudes] were mostly driven by political considerations."[2] Such generalizations are hard to maintain, since they must deal with thousands of authors and hundreds of scenarios, as Yang Shaoyun has pointed out in his examination of national-identity discourse in Tang and Song. Our task here is made simpler by the fact that we are asking about the presence of works, materials, ideas, and styles deemed alien in the midst of Chinese high culture, which gives us a shorter roster of phenomena to deal with. And in any case, culture deals with longer time-series. Works of art are usually designed to last, and the people who are making or reflecting on them don't have to answer the crises of the moment in the way that diplomats or officials do. Rather than uniform laws, perhaps we should first seek tendencies of group consciousness. On the other hand, culture (*wenhua* 文化) is often a register of sharper and more stubborn exclusions than political affiliation, ethnicity, geography, or even language provide. Defending or preserving culture, precisely because it is action in the realm of the Symbolic, invokes distinctions that may be impossible to draw clearly in material reality. Brindley has pointed to a sliding scale of rigor in the enforcement of the intellectual border, with the Ru insisting on the sharpest distinctions and hierarchical ranking between the customs of the Hua and the Yi—so great a gap that, as we saw from the debates among court Confucians, the customs of the Yi were not even recognizable as a ritual order and the music of the Yi, if it really was music, had to be led back to a Chinese origin.[3] Other streams of thought were not so strict: Buddhism, as everyone knows, came from abroad and was originally communicated in a "Hu language," and foreign music and even some poetry were adopted into the Chinese cultural repertoire. But texts encountered different fates according to their classification as Hua or Yi. Translated Buddhist texts were maintained and transmitted by institutions and specialists dedicated to them. But without any such support, the foreign-language texts of songs brought into the Chinese court became incomprehensible and vanished in the course of time, while Chinese-language texts that played variations on those texts were recopied and printed and so have survived. The making of a Hua/Yi distinction is an essential fact of Chinese cultural history. But that does not mean that the

distinction itself stands up to scrutiny. What is the difference between Hua and Yi, between Chinese and non-Chinese? Is there
a test?

Inevitably, the answers we propose to the question of what distinguishes the Hua and the Yi, and what defines the Hua, are
framed in particular situations and tend to reflect the preoccupa-
tions and limits of their times. I want first to turn back to a work of
ethnography from nearly a hundred years ago as a reminder of this
fact. Li Ji 李濟, who is best known today as the lead excavator of the
Anyang site and the founder of the archaeology department of Aca-
demia Sinica, received his PhD degree in anthropology at Harvard
with a thesis titled *The Formation of the Chinese People* (degree
awarded, 1923; publication in book form, 1928). Li Ji's investigation
is centered on the idea of a common descent group that has shared
physical features and a shared cultural repertoire. According to him,
the "descendants of the Yellow Emperor," signaled by a
"brachycephalic-leptorrhine" physical constitution (that is, broad
heads and narrow noses), are "the people who are found in, or
whose origin is traceable to, the land called China proper, and who
acknowledge their association with the making of Chinese history
from the beginning."[4] Li refers often to Jiang Tong's 江統 "Essay on
Expelling the Rong" 徙戎論, which I have mentioned earlier for its
attempt to enforce a strong separation between the Hua and the Yi.
The desire to identify once and for all the "Descendants of the
Yellow Emperor" and evaluate the degree of their mixing with
"Tungusic," "Tibeto-Burman," "Mon-Khmer," "Shan," "Hsiung-nu,"
"Mongol," and "Dwarf" elements in the Chinese population con-
joins several prominent strains in the discourse of Li's time: the
generally accepted lore of races as the ultimate actors of history, the
ethnic theme in the Han rejection of Manchu rule, Wilsonian ideals
of national self-government, and eugenicist classification and selection (of which one of Li's advisors, Earnest Hooton, was a pro-
ponent). There is not much left of this confluence of ideas today to
support pseudo-genetic definitions of identity. After publishing his
book, Li Ji abandoned them too.

The question of the difference between Hua and Yi—or better, the question of the pertinence of the difference between Hua and Yi—is tightly related to the question asked recently by Ge Zhaoguang 葛兆光 in *He wei Zhongguo?* 何為中國？ (What Is China?, 2014) and answered, in a fashion, by Ge's earlier book, *Zhai zi Zhongguo* 宅兹中國 (Residing in Zhongguo, 2011).[5] Ge Zhaoguang's question is mostly about the continuity and substantiality of the Chinese nation over time. Is it a discontinuous history, interrupted by invasions and radical changes of perspective, or does something transcend those divisions and endure throughout them? How must we define a nation so that it can possibly live up to both kinds of expectation, namely, that it will go on through time preserving the old and incorporating the new? In other words, what is the formula for its identity that will stand up to both kinds of historical testing? I surmise that one of the models for national existence that Ge has in mind is that of Ernest Renan, from his famous lecture "What Is a Nation?" of 1882. In that lecture Renan weighed the various answers that had been offered to that question and found them wanting. "Man is a slave neither of his race, his language, his religion, the course of his rivers, nor the direction of his mountain ranges."[6] That is, neither geography, religion, language, nor race suffices to form a nation. Of course Renan was thinking of France, which combines many populations formerly thought to be distinct—Celts and Latins and Germans and Basques, he might have enumerated; which has a majority religion, Catholicism, but admits many others; which certainly has a national language but began to enforce the teaching of it only after the Revolution of 1789; and the geographical frontiers of which had changed many times in recent memory. Moreover, the French nation of 1882 contained people of vastly different political orientations, from royalists to communists. Is it hopeless to lump all this diversity together as a single "nation"? Renan's solution is to say that a nation is, first, a matter of shared memory, the inventory of things that we in the present agree that "we" in the past have been and done; and second, a moral community, an agreement renewed every morning by the people inside it to go on living together. In putting forth that answer to the question of the historical persistence of the nation, Renan is letting democracy and education together have the last word. He is aware that the fabric of the moral community can all too easily tear. Civil wars erupt (one, the Paris Commune, had done so quite recently); provinces can demand independence; the population of an occupied area may feel wavering loyalties. One means of causing people to act in the interest of the nation they feel they belong to is to narrate history in such a way that such actions make sense. Let's put ourselves in the shoes of an Alsatian Protestant in 1871, just after Alsace and Lorraine have been snatched away from France by the victorious Prussians. In an effort to persuade me that the French have never been my community, someone may whisper in my ear that "France" was responsible for the St. Bartholomew's Day Massacre in 1572, the Revocation of the Edict of Nantes in 1685, and associated horrors. If I still feel myself loyal to Paris and the Republic, I might dismiss such arguments by contending that it wasn't "France" that murdered the Huguenots in 1572, it was a mob stirred up by unscrupulous factional leaders; it wasn't "France" that expelled the Protestants and Jews in 1685, but Louis XIV, led on by his mistress and his confessor. In other words, if you don't mind my devising this imaginary scenario, the narration of history leads us to remember certain things and to forget or dismiss certain other things, as a way of taking responsibility together with others for the things remembered and denying involvement in the things that must be forgotten. "Forgetting, and I would even add historical error, is essential to the formation of a nation. . . . Every French citizen is obliged to forget the St. Bartholomew's Day Massacre and the campaigns against the Catharists in twelfth-century Provence."[7]

To this model of the nation as a pattern held in memory and renewed every day by the rituals of teaching and narrating—the *Places of Memory* described by Pierre Nora and his associates—Ge Zhaoguang has a complicated response.[8]

和歐洲不同，中國的政治疆域和文化空間是從中心向邊緣
彌漫開來的，即使不說三代，從秦漢時代起，「車同軌，書同
文，行同倫，」語言文字、倫理風俗和政治制度開始把民族
在這個空間中逐漸固定下來，這與歐洲認為「民族原本就是
人類史上晚近的新現象」不同，因此，把傳統帝國與現代國
家區分為兩個世代的理論，並不符合中國歷史，也不符合中
國的國家意識觀念和國家生成歷史。9

Unlike in Europe, the political territory and cultural space of
China spread gradually from the center to the peripheries; leaving aside the "Three Ages" [of semilegendary history], from the
Qin and Han eras on, "cart tracks were of the same width, writing used the same characters, morals followed the same rules,"
and language and writing, moral customs, and political institutions began gradually to stabilize the nation in this space. This
is quite different from the European understanding that "the
nation is a recent phenomenon in human history." For this reason, the theory that divides traditional empires and modern
states into different time periods does not correspond to Chinese history, nor does it correspond to the Chinese consciousness of the state or the history of the formation of the state.[10]

Now this China, radiating outward from the center, is just one
of the many possible Chinas. It is the China visible to those who
put themselves at the meridian of the "Dao tong" 道統, a bit like
the solstice sunrise as it appears to an observer who stands at the
right spot among the pillars of Stonehenge. The title of Ge's 2011
book points up the ambiguity I am trying to bring into focus. *Zhai
zi Zhongguo*, as translated by Jesse Field and Qin Fang, has been
published in English as *Here in 'China' I Dwell*. As always with
translation, the translators have had to make a few decisions and
exclude some possibilities. Putting "China" between quotation
marks suggests a questioning of static identities, but the translators' rendition of the title phrase still leaves little room for the
range of histories that need to be narrated and represented if we
are going to understand the process of production of China at all.

The quotation that makes up the book's title does not assume the existence of any such thing as "China." It might be better reflected by *Dwelling in the Central States*, or (more verbosely) *Dwelling in the Central States That Would Become China.* "Would become": history as anticipation of the present. For Ge Zhaoguang, the problem is how to explain China; China is the given fact, and its process of development the thing that must be reconstructed. The title phrase may seem to announce the fact, but on closer inspection it alludes to the process. It comes from an eleventh-century BCE bronze vessel famous for containing, as some would put it, the first occurrence of the words "Zhongguo" 中國. It reads as follows: 隹武王既克大邑商。則廷告于天曰。余期宅茲中或，自茲乂民 "King Wu conquered the great city Shang. Then he made a courtyard announcement to heaven, saying: 'Henceforth I shall reside in this central territory [*zhai zi zhong huo (sic)*], and from here shall I govern my subordinates.'"[11] Although the He *zun* inscription is often said to be the earliest testimony to the phrase *Zhongguo*, the phrase's second character as cast in the bronze is not simply the present-day character *guo* 國. It looks, instead, like *huo* 或, a word that in later written Chinese came to mean roughly "someone" or "either." The Han-dynasty lexicographer Xu Shen 許慎 in fact lists 或 as the etymon and treats 域 ("region"), 𨻂 (also "region"; no longer in use), and our present word 國 as equivalent words.[12] 國, it seems, may well have been invented to distinguish the meaning "kingdom, country" from its near synonyms a thousand or so years after the inscriber of the He *zun* wrote (or did s/he?) "Zhongguo." Sarah Allan takes the *huo* to be equivalent to *yu* 域, "region" or "territory": thus her translation, "in this central territory."

Even to frame the alternative puts us in the position of anticipating a history in which *huo* 或 would be distinct from *guo* 國, and *guo* 國 would have to be determined as singular—"China"—or plural—"the Central States." The former is a lexicographical or paleographical problem; the second, a historical or political one. But it is not so easy to disentangle etymology from history. Perhaps this is a typically Chinese problem. But it is a problem for us,

The He *zun* inscription from Tang Lan, "He zun mingwen jieshi," *Wenwu* 1976.1, 62.

standing where we do among the outcomes of a history that, at the time the bronze was cast, lay entirely in the future, in potentiality and undifferentiation.

The Chinese language allows Ge to suspend the resolution of the ambiguity of 中國 / 或 / 域 as being, in reference to the multistate system of preimperial East Asia, "the Central States" or "the Central Territories," and as becoming something more like "China" in later periods of unified rule and cultural selfidentification. It is like a pun with a three-thousand-year delay. But when we translate Ge's words into English, we have to choose one or the other meaning on every occurrence; there's no room for ambiguity. Only anachronism can make the

Detail of the He *zun* inscription

Zhongguo of the eleventh-century BCE inscription equivalent to the *Zhongguo* on present-day coins and passports. The purpose of Ge Zhaoguang's book is actually not to enforce this anachronism but to follow the evolving meanings of "Zhongguo" and related terms through history, asking again and again whether a stable or enduring reality corresponds to the reiterated terms. Ge's solution is to hold that "China has always had a clear and stable center, even if its margins have at times been vague and unstable."[13] Other historians may see the center as wobbling; that is the historians' point of contention, and we do not need to resolve it as a matter of translation. But to translate this fluctuating or plural "Zhongguo" uniformly as "China" obliterates the question by answering it prematurely. In this English translation, Ge Zhaoguang comes across as more dogmatic than he is in Chinese.

This is not to say that Ge Zhaoguang does not occasionally reason backward from China as it stands today to earlier territorial, political, and cultural structures. In these matters there is a constant temptation to take what actually happened as what had to happen. We must, I think, be wary of teleology. Ge Zhaoguang's studies are an exercise in historical epistemology: he looks back to scholars and rulers of the past who had an answer to the question of what China is and argues that, for all the variety of their definitions of China, they have a common conceptual basis.

How do things look from the other side? From one of the other sides?

As has often been observed, Chinese writing is inseparable from Chinese identity. The Uyghur historian Kahar Barat 卡哈爾· 巴拉提 puts it rather bluntly:

> 其實是漢字制造出了漢民族，沒有這個字就沒有漢民族。漢民族本來是一百多個民族同化成一體的。這個過程還在繼續。中國有 56 個民族，過五十年可能只剩 6 個民族了。其實現在就有一半已經有名無實了。[14]

Chinese characters were really what brought about the Han ethnicity; without these characters there would be no Han ethnicity. The Han ethnicity really is just over a hundred peoples assimilated into one body. This process is still continuing. China had 56 ethnicities [officially speaking, on the basis of the 1954 report on *minzu*]; after another fifty years have gone by there will probably be only 6 left. In fact, at present half of them exist in name only.

I think I detect a bit of sarcasm in Barat's remarks, but what he says is by no means absurd. As Xi Jinping might say, the creation of the Chinese script is a "mighty accomplishment of the great Chinese people"—but it is equally defensible to say that the great Chinese people is a mighty accomplishment of the Chinese script.[15] One way that the Han ethnicity has grown is by absorbing neighboring peoples into it, and one way it has done so is by schooling those peoples in the Hanzi 漢字 writing system.

It's a widespread story. In Australia, or South America, or Brittany, or wherever you look, there is a similar receding frontier of local languages. The children start to learn the dominant language of education and professional life and neglect the language of their parents and grandparents. Before long the villages contain only a few old people who still speak it, and in the best of cases someone then realizes that it's urgent to send in linguists and ethnographers. Samples of the language may be salvaged. Perhaps even a grammar and dictionary can be compiled. Maybe someone will set up schools to restore the language to life by teaching it to the young.

The unequal contest of languages sponsored by powerful states and those spoken by powerless, loosely organized communities is a global epidemic of language disappearance.[16] The thing about China is that this has been going on for many centuries. The Uyghur historian cannot but be aware that opportunities for getting an education and a livelihood for people in Xinjiang and Gansu are increasingly pinned to competence in Putonghua, and the Turkic languages of the region are accordingly fading away. This is certainly by design.[17] But China's northern and western borderlands present a somewhat unusual case of language extinction, because not only spoken language is at stake, but written language as well. At the indicated point in Kahar Barat's conversation with Wang Lixiong just quoted, the topic is the Sixteen Kingdoms era and the arrival of Chinese-language Buddhist scriptures to the Uyghur kingdoms, which had already been Buddhist for centuries and would not be Islamicized for several centuries more: so the topic is not just the linguistic, religious, and ethnic contentions of today, but a much longer competition among the languages of literary culture. The Old Uyghur writing system dates approximately back to the Tang, before it was replaced by Persian Arabic writing, the Cyrillic and Roman alphabets, and Chinese character transliteration, depending on the region and the moment. Xinjiang ranks with Vietnam as an area of extraordinary script variance; both areas are sites of intercultural contact and zones of repeated conquest. So when Barat indicates, with a touch of bitter humor, the case of those "minority nationalities" that exist now "in name only," as a stamp on someone's identity card, he must be thinking of the steep odds against the survival of Turkic Uyghur cultural practices under the "fifty-six nationalities" policy.

To focus on the Chinese character rather than the Mandarin language or Putonghua adds an important degree of precision. People of many distinct linguistic groups were absorbed into the body of Han ethnicity through the diffusion of dialects other than Mandarin over the course of history, for example the Bai, Yi, and Zhuang, who came into contact with speakers of southern dialects, or the original inhabitants of the Fujian coast. The Yue eventually saw their state annexed by Chu, and the language of Chu, however it differed from the language of the Central States, comes down to us in standard written Sinitic form. The writing of some things brings obliteration of others. "People without history," a phrase typically used to refer to indigenous populations, are sometimes people whose history has been erased or replaced.[18] Ian Hacking has often insisted on the performative power of labels and categories, holding that the discovery of a fact creates it. In particular, proclaiming a fact about human beings initiates a feedback loop between those humans' representations and their realities (two provisional categories that cannot be held apart for long). He suggests there that when a new label for a form of human behavior or identity is created, it can draw people into acting out those identities: once you are able to conceive of yourself as a split personality, an empath, or a Scorpio, you may begin doing all the things that are done by people in those categories. The label licenses a form of behavior that was not cognitively available to people before the category was invented.[19] Just so, spreading the news about such identities as "subject of the Emperor," "monk," or "Confucian scholar" amounted to making up people who would inhabit those labels. But in weakened border communities, "Making People Up" goes together with "Taking People Away," that is, rendering former categories no longer inhabitable.

Can script "make people up"? Zhang Binglin 章炳麟 (Zhang Tai-yan 章太炎, 1869–1936), in a polemical essay advocating the overthrow of the Qing dynasty and the expulsion of Manchus as an alien race, clearly took script to be a form of identity, arguing that

> 則滿日皆為黃種。而日為同族。滿非同族。載在歷史。粲然可知。 ... 則日本先有漢字。而後制作和文。今雖襍用。漢字有居大半。至滿洲則自有清書。形體絕異。

Both the Manchus and the Japanese belong to the yellow race, but as can be clearly seen from history the Japanese are of the same ethnicity [as ourselves], while the Manchus are not. . . . Japan first used Han [Chinese] characters, and later developed the Japanese script. Although now both are used together, Han [Chinese] characters still occupy more than half of what is written. The Manchus, on the other hand, have their own writing whose form is completely different.[20]

A fifteenth-century Korean official voiced a similar concern for script as identity in a memorial expressing reservations about the adoption of the now-standard *han'gul* phonetic system: "Only such peoples as the Mongolians, Tanguts, Jurchens, Japanese, and Tibetans have their own writings. But this is a matter that involves the barbarians and is unworthy of our concern."[21]

A script is never just marks on paper. What letters you write define who you can communicate with (at a distance at least), and your communicative networks define who you are. Writing in Chinese for a bilingual subject may eventually become writing exclusively in Chinese and shaping your writing for the public that writes and reads in Chinese. A process of coevolution, of intertwined causalities, links sign systems and personal identities.[22]

Ge Zhaoguang and Kahar Barat are telling a similar story, but from different ends; this is the "asymmetry" referred to in the title of this chapter. It is the story of the expansion of Chinese culture from center to margins. One most often hears this story told from the center's point of view, only rarely from that of the margin. The conventional name for the center's version of the story is "Sinicization," *hanhua* 漢化. Chinese friends occasionally commend my *hanhua*, and I take it as a compliment; like most compliments, it involves some exaggeration.

The "gradual spread from the center to the peripheries" evoked by Ge may suggest an inexorable, anonymous, linear process. For protagonists of the expansion itself, however, it was anything but inevitable; it was, rather, a civilizing mission that demanded effort and a militant consciousness. Parts of previous

Chinese territory from time to time fell out of the control of the legitimate dynasty or failed to follow the model of the Central States. Advocates of Central States culture would then call for a recovery operation.[23] Such episodes of reconquest and rearmament are frequent in Chinese history. Writing in the fifteenth century, that is, shortly after the Ming dynasty had replaced the Yuan conquerors, Qiu Jun 丘濬 (1421–1495) was acutely sensitive to such reversals. His *Daxue yanyi bu* 大學衍義補 (Supplement to an extended commentary on the "Great Learning"), a work of statecraft addressed to the Ming sovereign, includes in its chapter on "transformation through teaching" many narratives of primary conversion and reconversion by tireless Confucian administrators. Exemplary tales are told of the introduction of culture to a place that is simply wild and barbarous, such as this one:

文翁為蜀郡守, 仁愛好教化, 見蜀地僻陋有蠻夷風, 文翁欲誘進之, 乃選郡縣小吏開敏有才者親自飭厲, 遣詣京師受業博士, 數歲皆成就還歸, 文翁以為右職。...縣是大化, 蜀郡學者比齊、魯焉。[24]

When Wen Weng [156–101 BCE] supervised the commandery of Shu [in present Sichuan Province], he was generous, kind, and devoted to moral teaching. He saw that the area of Shu was backward and provincial, with customs of the Man and Yi, and he decided to lead it to improvement. So he chose the most intelligent and able of the lesser officials in the commandery and sent them to the capital at his own expense to take instruction from renowned scholars. After a few years they returned with attainments, and Wen Weng took them as his advisors. . . . In this way he greatly transformed Shu, so that it produced scholars on a par with even [the states of] Qi and Lu [—the homelands of Confucius and Mencius].

That is the civilizing mission in action.[25] In places that have undergone centuries of alien rule, Qiu Jun goes on to tell us, energetic disinfection measures are now required:

漢之時異端之教猶未甚熾，今去其時千年矣，世變愈下而佛、道
二教大為斯民之蠱惑，非明古禮以正人心、息邪說，則民財愈
匱而民性愈蕩矣。[26]

In the time of the Han, heretical teachings were not so flagrant.
We now live 1,500 years later, and the world has lost its senses,
so that the two religions of Buddhism and Daoism pester and
abuse the people. If we fail to illuminate the ancient rituals that
rectify the hearts of people and extinguish evil ideas, the commoners' wealth will grow ever more depleted and their character ever more debauched.

後魏封回為安州刺史，山民願樸，父子賓旅同寢一室，回下車勸
令別處，其俗遂改。
臣按：今所謂中州之域漸染金、元之風，猶有同炕之俗。其為
治化之累大矣，請痛禁之。[27]

Feng Hui of the Later Wei became Reminder of Anzhou, where
the mountaineers were extremely unrefined. Fathers, sons, and
passing travelers all slept in one room. Hui got off his carriage
and urged them to find separate places. Their habit changed
instantly.

[Note by Qiu Jun:] Your servant comments: Nowadays the so-
called Zhongzhou Valley is contaminated by Jurchen and Mongol habits. People still sleep on a single heated brick bed. The
hindrance to good governance and moral transformation is great
indeed. I request that such habits be vigorously suppressed.

Qiu Jun's program for cultural transformation involves vigorous
direction from the center, in response to the signs that the outlying
districts have forgotten to what civilization they belong.

臣按：天下之風俗未必皆美也，人君之教化未必皆及也，蓋輿
圖之廣，廣谷大川異製，民生其間異俗。人君一人不能一一躬
歷之，而其所為條教又未必皆能一一如其俗，是以有賴於承
流宣化之吏，隨其地因其俗以倡率教導之，若文翁之治蜀者
是已。[28]

Your servant comments: It is by no means the case that manners and morals are good everywhere. Nor do all the reforming efforts of rulers reach universally. For in the breadth of the great world there are places divided by rivers and valleys, with the result that they have different regulations, and the people there have different customs. The ruler is but one individual and cannot go to every place personally, and the educational proclamations that he makes will not necessarily fit the circumstances of each place. This is why he makes use of locally informed officials who can according to place and custom guide the people to follow his transformation, just as Wen Weng did for Sichuan.

The whole point is to overcome the differences of places and customs, if necessary by acknowledging them at first. With an adequate number of well-informed and correctly minded officials, the Imperial Way can be extended to new territories and new "native speakers" of the ritual and moral codes of the center created.

Qiu Jun tells only stories of success in pursuing the "civilizing mission"; at worst there are areas that have temporarily fallen out of civilization, but they can be recovered. His model of history is one of ongoing cultural integration under imperial Ruist auspices. Of course Qiu Jun is aware that the civilizing mission can falter, as it had done under the Song and the Yuan. The recommendations he makes in his work of history and statecraft are meant to guard against the possibility of that happening again.

People who are aware of the multicultural character of China often write the history of China in what Hayden White would designate the mode of comedy, of reconciliation: at the outset of the story, there are differences and conflicts, but in the end the differences are resolved into a unity or harmony and everyone is better off than they were in the state of conflict.[29] In such stories, it usually falls to the Confucian scholar-official tradition, exactly the tradition embodied by Qiu Jun, to synthesize the divergent traditions. Take, for example, Li Zehou's 李澤厚 *The Chinese*

Aesthetic Tradition (*Huaxia meixue* 華夏美學): "Whether in real life or at the level of thought and the emotions," he says, "it is the tradition of Confucius and Mencius that has proved the mainstay of generations of intellectuals in China"; in all dynasties, "it was the Confucian-educated scholar-intellectuals who produced almost all of Chinese philosophy, aesthetics, art, and literature." Daoism and Buddhism, in Li's conception of Chinese intellectual history, are always "absorbed" into the Confucian mainstream.[30] Primitive and marginal ethnicities have their part to play too: "Early totemic/shamanistic Chinese culture laid the foundation for the unity of sense and reason, nature and society, that *would come to* characterize the Chinese aesthetic tradition" (2; emphasis mine). The emotional, participatory, immediately vivid culture of Chu and the far South contributed essential resources to the maturing of Chinese artistic sensibility, in Li's view (25, 28, 159). The minor, alien or marginal traditions are "absorbed"; they do not absorb the mainstream, in this style of narration, or even durably contest it. Of course, the natives of Chu or Yue could have had no idea that they were destined to contribute to moderating the ethical strictness of the northern tradition; the combination of the two is a retrospective teleological construction. The formula is ever-popular. I quote from another recent synthetic work: "Chinese civilization resulted from the gradual fusion of multiple sources. . . . However, the Yellow River Valley culture obviously played a dominant role." "Harsh living conditions" in the North compelled the members of that culture to "gather their dispersed people together into large and powerful communities"; thus "the ideology of the state reached maturity there far earlier than in other regions." On the other hand—that deterministic, logically required other hand—"In the Yangtze valley, the climate was hot and humid. . . . It was relatively easy to lead a simple existence there. Consequently, even though there was a similar need to form large, powerful communities, it was . . . by no means as pressing as that in the north. Thus, in the Yangtze valley . . . the ideology to preserve social order and strengthen community power through restraining the individual was not as well developed as that in the north." In the culture of the North, "music, dance and singing were regarded as the means to regulate community life and to carry out an ethical purpose. . . . The main functions of the arts of Chu are represented, however, in providing the satisfaction of aesthetic pleasure, and in this way [they] fully display the dynamism of human emotions."[31] Chinese culture emerges as the reconciliation of North and South, but under the watchful eye and social conscience of the North. In such tellings, the northern culture of the Central States expands to "absorb" and digest what it needs from the culture of the South, perhaps being modified by it in some particulars but not in its essence. It is never the case that the culture of the Central States is absorbed by anything else.

These narratives are end-driven: they explain the past by the results attained in the present, they make the present appear as a legitimate, nay inevitable, consequence of developments in the past, and they present diversity under the aegis of harmonization, such that the warring elements of the past are now necessary ingredients in a new synthesis, that is, the national culture. Alexander Beecroft has detected a parallel in the constitution of the high-culture textual traditions in ancient Greece and ancient China, to wit, the Homeric poems and the *Shijing*: the canons start from local expressions with local publics, are progressively added to and reconfigured to reflect a wider geographical area, a bigger pantheon, a larger roster of dialects, and eventually become "panchoric," that is, they draw from and are current in the whole cultural domain of the Greek-speaking and Chinese-speaking worlds, respectively.[32] I suspect that the larger purpose of such anthology-like compositions is to train us in "seeing like a state": to put the epichoric inside the panchoric, to see the local as predecessor of the global and not the other way around, or some other combination of the elements.

National literary traditions are carefully developed expressions of a teleology. Behind them is a narrative of expansion and harmonization. And national literary and cultural histories, to come back to my main subject, are constructed in the same way. Their perspective is what cosmologists might call anthropic: since we are the products of the process, can we doubt that it happened in this way or question whether it ought to have?[33] We, the people of nation *N*, looking back on the history and literary monuments of *N*, recognize ourselves in them and imagine that their protagonists would recognize us. But to the reconciliations of comedy, there must correspond, at least for some observers and in some localities, a tragic narrative of loss. The speakers of the Yue language, the followers of unacknowledged religious canons, the people whose languages or scripts have fallen out of use rarely have a word in the discussion. Is it impossible to recover their lost voices?

Rarely. At points in the major tradition, however, a tragic sense of the fragility of majority culture is heard. Sometimes it seems that the Way is about to perish. Du Fu's 杜甫 poems of the An Lushan 安祿山 rebellion and the Tibetan sack of Chang'an in 763 exemplify this fear: everyone who has read Du Fu will remember his desperate struggle to keep body and soul together and to ensure the survival of his family while fleeing the disasters of war and constantly noting down the apocalyptic signs of the near-collapse of the Tang dynasty's world order. One poem, written in the depths of the rebellion, goes so far as to prescribe a halt in the eternal civilizing mission:

幽薊餘蛇豕，乾坤尚虎狼。
諸侯春不貢，使者日相望。
慎勿吞青海，無勞問越裳。
大君先息戰，歸馬華山陽。

In Youzhou and Jizhou, serpents and boars remain,
Heaven and earth are still with tigers and wolves.
The lords of domains send no spring tribute,
A string of court envoys stare at each other daily.
Take care not to try to swallow up Kokonor,
Don't trouble yourself to ask about Yuechang.
May our great ruler be the first to cease battle,
Bring the horses back to graze on the sunlit side of Mount
    Hua.[34]

"Serpents and boars" (*shetun* 蛇豕), "tigers and wolves" (*hulang* 虎狼), "jackals and wolves" (*chailang* 豺狼), "poisonous serpents" (*dushe* 毒蛇), "ravening tigers" (*menghu* 猛虎), "the Rong curs" (*quanrong* 犬戎): such are Du Fu's choice epithets for the Tibetan, Sogdian, and Uyghur armies occupying different parts of the Chinese realm.[35] The point is not to chide Du Fu for offensive language but to make clear how our empathy for Du Fu relies on sharing his perception of China as a precious pearl trampled by swine. A certain dehumanization of the enemy goes together with the best traditions of humanism. The vassal lords are no longer sending their spring tribute to Chang'an, perhaps because the roads are blocked, or perhaps because they are waiting to learn if a new dynasty is about to be declared (if so, the new overlord will receive the homage). In yamens and offices, those who show up for work stare at each other blankly with nothing to do. Du Fu urges the emperor to repress his martial urge to "swallow up Kokonor" or Qinghai—an absurd directive, because the emperor is in flight and Qinghai is securely held by the Tuyuhun allies of the Tibetans. (Yes, those same Tuyuhuns whose history began with two competing brothers and some stubborn horses.[36]) It's a discreet, counterfactual reminder of the fact that "projecting power" is no longer an option. Even less pertinent, at this moment, is concern about the condition of Yuechang, that is, Vietnam, in the far South, a land from which the Duke of Zhou once received emissaries in confirmation of the sagely charisma of his rule. Du Fu expresses the wish that Tang Daizong can, like King Wu after the conquest of the Shang and the proclamation of the Zhou Dynasty, put the war horses out to pasture as a sign that he plans no future military campaigns now that his victory is complete. A flattering parallel, and quite absurd given that the Tang was in the position of having to sue for peace, not proclaim victory, and might well be entirely defeated. The Tibetans, when they entered the capital of Chang'an, had installed a new emperor, a relative of the Jincheng Princess mentioned earlier who was the consort of the Tibetan king, and they seemed to expect to rule Tang China indirectly through him. Du Fu's poem is con-trafactual advice. Not that this message, fictively addressed to Tang Daizong, would ever have reached him, but Du Fu's courtly indirectness verges on flattery and absurdity. It amounts to a list of the elements of the imperial civilizing mission, inventoried and systematically negated. No longer can the legitimate Tang sover-eign send troops out to guard the borders, receive tribute from subordinate states, command officials to execute policies, or de-clare peace and war. The poem prescribes a tremendous and tragic backing-down from centuries of precedent.

The combats of the An Lushan rebellion are, of course, respon-sible for many pages in the Tang poetry anthologies and in the historical texts devoted to casting blame for the capital's fall. Is it all Emperor Xuanzong's fault, An Lushan's fault, or Yang Guo-zhong's, or Yang Guifei's, or Guo Ziyi's, and so forth? Does the error lie in badly executed policies, or improper nominations, or the commissioning of foreign generals in border areas, or a thoughtless policy toward foreign states? The Tang histories and analytic works like *Zizhi tongjian* 資治通鑑 (The comprehensive mirror for aid in governing) abound with competing accounts of what went wrong but, most of all, express the judgment that the events were so exceptional, so aberrant, that they must prompt thorough soul-searching, house-cleaning, and preemptive reform. On the Tibetan side, however, the narratives are much simpler:

Generally, when harmony prevailed in the successive appear-ance of kings and emperors, nephew and uncle [i.e., Tibet and China], then there was a mutual exchange of presents between the royal houses; and when discord reigned, they would mutu-ally wage war against one another; suchlike incidents could be cited in great number. . . . During the regency of the Tibetan king Khri-lde btsug-btsan Mes Ag-tshoms . . . the daughter of the [Chinese] emperor, Princess Jincheng, arrived in Tibet [in 710]. As dowry, the daughter was given many tens of thou-sands of pieces of fine silk, manuals of every sort of techniques in the art of craftsmanship and all sorts of paraphernalia and provisions for journeying. . . . The territories of Liangzhou and Xiazhou were controlled by Tibet for a period of thirty years. In the time of his son . . . there were disagreements between nephew [i.e., Tibet] and uncle [i.e., China], wherefore wars in turn actually were waged numerous times. Zhang rGya-tsha lha-snang and general lHa-bzang khlu-dpal, etc., leading a Tibetan army of twenty thousand soldiers, conquered Lintao, Taochou, and the territories of Manzi. Thereafter the nephew and uncle exchanged presents. . . . Accordingly, mNga'-bdag Ral-pa-can also, with a period of hostility between uncle and nephew, [led] an army of tens of thousands of soldiers, whereafter China was invaded, and all provincial fortified garrisons were conquered. The Chinese monks and Tibetan chaplains acted as mediators and oath-witnesses, the Chinese [were] compelled to offer presents to please the nephew, and henceforth it was agreed that no hostility was to prevail.[37]

A circuit of communication grounds a moral community. When addressing such a community, one adopts its rules. The rules whereby the history narrated by and for Tibetans makes sense are transactional: gifts are given or withheld, amity or hostility follows, and when hostility is the prevailing climate, war is prosecuted until presents are made once more. The occupation of Chang'an is just one in a series of similar events, with no cosmic implications at all. The *Old Tibetan Annals* are even briefer and do not engage in the search for pattern in international relations. There it is simply recorded that the Tibetan generals "led a military campaign to the capital and sacked the capital. The Lord of China fled, another Lord of China was newly appointed, and the military campaign returned."[38] The tragedy passes as quickly as "downing three cups of wine."[39]

The Tibetan chroniclers and Du Fu may be parsing the same history, but they bring to it vastly different grammars of action, obligation, role, and causality. When seen from the outside,

without its theoretical basis, the Chinese civilizing mission re-
solves into an unreliable stream of gifts and offenses. Every now
and then one has to raise an army to restore the flow of gifts, or
maybe sack the capital. This narrative does not, at least, consent
to "harmonization" from the "center." The two styles of narrative
collide, asymmetrically, in an event and its imputed meanings.

Confronting the outside means confronting the possibility that
one's devices for making meaning in the world are no longer op-
erative. Reporting on and seeking to master such feelings is the
concern of Chinese exiles—involuntary emissaries from the
center—over many centuries. What kinds of meanings were they
able to make for themselves while standing at what must have
been for them the edge of the world, with little confidence in the
progress of "all history . . . toward one great goal"?[40]

5

Exiles and Emissaries amid Their New Neighbors: The View from the Edge of the World

「咨爾漢黎，均是一民」：在世界邊緣上

THE "GREAT LEARNING" says: "Only the benevolent man is capable of banishing [unreliable officials], sending them to live among the barbarians of the four quarters rather than dwelling with those in the Central States" 唯仁人放流之，迸諸四夷，不與同中國.[1] One way that participants in Chinese high culture made contact with the cultures of surrounding peoples was through exile. The court used its powers of nomination to remove a troublesome official or the leader of a quarreling faction from the capital. In so doing, at the same time it continued the consolidation of its control in the borderlands and, as an added convenience, exposed the disgraced official to the risk of death from tropical diseases. A famous story concerns an official who was so afraid of banishment that he refused to have even a map of the South in his official quarters; sure enough, he eventually fell out of favor and received the summons to pack his bags and go to a remote tropical prefecture; he died on the way.[2] The most available English terms for this practice, "exile" and "banishment," as usual do not quite correspond to the reality. For it is not across a border and into a foreign jurisdiction that the erring official is sent, but to a distant and untrodden part of the same empire, there to prod and hector some of the emperor's least promising candidates for civilization. Language, or rather the lack of a common language, is a frequent theme in the "long tradition of southern strangeness."[3] Han Yu describes living in one of those desolate places.

縣郭無居民，官無丞尉，夾江荒茅篁竹之間，小吏十餘家，皆鳥言夷面。始至，言語不通，畫地為字，然後可告以出租賦，奉期約。是以賓客遊從之士，無所為而至。[4]

In the county seat there are no permanent residents [i.e., settlers], and the garrison is unstaffed. At the bend of the river, surrounded by reeds and tall bamboos, is an outpost ringed by ten or so houses of tribal clerks whose language is birdlike and whose faces are savage. When I arrived, we had no words in common, and the most I could do was scratch lines on the ground in the guise of characters; thereby I was able to order them to collect ground rent and taxes and enforce contracts. There is no reason for anyone to come here, whether as guests or colleagues.

You might as well converse with a crocodile—a beast whose proper place is "among the Man and Yi who dwell in Chu and Yue" 蠻夷楚越.[5] Liu Zongyuan 柳宗元 describes his arrival among the Dong 峒 people of Liuzhou 柳州, his final place of exile in Guangxi, in these verses:

郡城南下接通津，異服殊音不可親 . . .
愁向公庭問重譯，欲投章甫作文身。[6]

Going south from the prefecture, you come to a ford and
crossroads,
But the clothing is different, the words are strange, there is
no possibility of connection. . . .
With a heavy heart I face the audience hall and must rely
on a translator.
I might as well throw away my cap of office and join the
tattooed savages.

The final line, with its reminiscence of the *Zhuangzi* story about the futility of trying to sell Confucian ceremonial caps to natives who shave their heads and go about naked with tattooed skin, is an expression of utter frustration at the hopelessness of the task. "I am held prisoner on the border of Chu and Yue," he laments, "remote and cut off from the Central Plains" 余囚楚越之交極兮，邈離絕乎中原.[7] His situation is hardly less perilous than that of the sea merchants who, as they sail toward lands of "black-toothed natives whose limbs are tattooed with scale patterns" 黑齒鱗文肌, risk being eaten by sea monsters of various spiky and toothy kinds.[8] And indeed, although Liu Zongyuan's southern exiles (to Yongzhou in present-day Hunan, 805–814; to Liuzhou in present-day Guangxi, 815–819) are generally thought to have introduced a period of new creative energy, it is hard to describe his residence in those areas as anything but a challenge that provoked; it is not quite a prospect that inspired. His celebrated "Yongzhou baji" 永州八記 (Eight records of Yongzhou) describe the landscape of one of his remote postings but scarcely indicate a human trace.[9] The "Exposition on a Snake Catcher" 捕蛇者說 raises a general problem—the burden of excessive taxes—and only the snakes are specific to the region.[10] "The Mice of the Man from Yong" 永某氏之鼠 is a fable.[11] Liu's letters from his places of banishment concern friends in the capital, current policy debates, occasionally his own feelings of isolation and melancholy—but from these writings the local populations and their customs are absent.[12] Only the descriptions of landscape remain to fix the site of Liu Zongyuan's fourteen years of exile. But it is an uninhabited landscape of rocks, ponds, and trees.

This was the state of mind of the classic Tang exiles. Living among people with whom they could not talk and having no interest in those people except as the recipients of their administrative decrees, Han Yu and Liu Zongyuan conducted their social life in letters to and from friends in the capital. Indeed, in Liu Zongyuan's letters and essays from exile, more space is given to the poisonous insects and snakes of southern Hunan than to the tattooed human inhabitants.[13]

When Su Shi's opposition to Wang Anshi's reforms earned him a second exile in 1097, it was to the island of Hainan, at the time no vacation spot but a malaria-ridden, open-air dungeon. Outwardly, this might seem like a repetition of the fates of Han Yu and Liu Zongyuan. But Su never did anything like other people. Old, sick, but never completely discouraged, Su Shi invented a new identity for himself on Hainan: "I am a Hainanese," he says, 我本海南民, and furthermore, "Hearken, ye Han and Li! / We are but one people!" 咨爾漢黎，均是一民. The poems and prefaces in his collection from that exile, *Haiwai ji* 海外集, speak of his friendships with some of these Li people, the original inhabitants of the island, and show him lingering with his neighbors over a few cups of their home-brewed liquor.[14] These locals have names: Li Ziyun 黎子雲 and "the Lis" 諸黎. Su, the former prefect of Hangzhou, goes out "half-sober and half-drunk to pay a call on the Lis" 半醒半醉問諸黎; responsible for his state is a brew prepared "in the manner of the unassimilated Li, with dry ferment in a wide-bellied crock" 小酒生黎法，乾糟瓦盎中.[15] Some of the Li can converse with him in Chinese; some are Su Shi's students; others are illiterate locals speaking only the aboriginal language. Su Shi had his son Guo 過 with him, so his isolation was not total. Still, one doesn't imagine Han Yu or Liu Zongyuan reporting this kind of random wandering through the cow pastures:

被酒獨行遍至子雲威徽先覺四黎之舍三首

（一）
半醒半醉問諸黎，　竹刺藤梢步步迷。
但尋牛矢覓歸路，　家在牛欄西復西。
（二）
總角黎家三小童，　口吹蔥葉送迎翁。
莫作天涯萬里意，　溪邊自有舞雩風。
（三）
符老風情老奈何，　朱顏減盡鬢絲多。
投梭每困東鄰女，　換扇唯逢春夢婆。[16]

*Wandering Alone While Tipsy, I Stop at the Houses of Four
Lis (Ziyun, Wei, Hui, and Xianjue): Three Poems*

1

Somewhere between drunk and sober, I go off to visit the
   Lis,
But amid bamboo spikes and wisteria branches I get more
   bewildered with every step.
My only means of finding the way home is to track the cow
   patties:
Where I live is west of the cattle shed, and yet further west.

2

Three or four Li children with hair bound up in horns
Razz with scallion stalks to salute and dismiss this
   old man.
Let no one long for some realm ten thousand miles off.
This creekside is the dancing at the rain sacrifice.

3

Candidate Fu, still flirtatious at your advanced age!
Your rosy cheeks have drained away, your temples are
   mostly white.
Having had your teeth knocked out by the beautiful
   woman next door,
It's time you bought a new fan and went to see Old Mother
   "Spring Dream."

Drunk, lost, and on his way to an undistinguished lodging, Su
Shi cannot take himself too seriously. The line "This creekside is
the dancing at the rain sacrifice" alludes to a passage in the *Analects*
(11.26) where Confucius confesses that a good river bath with
some young friends and a walk past the rain altars appeals to him
more than wealth, office, or ceremony. This unusual moment—
the Sage vouching for simple pleasures—lets the banished official
pose as beachcomber, refusing to pine for life in the capital. In the
third poem, Su Shi finds an alter ego in another Hainan character,
Old Fu, reportedly a failed examination candidate who could not

stop pursuing women. Whether the "beautiful woman next door" is really a woman or an allegory for worldly success, she is no more receptive to Fu's advances than was the neighbor of Xie Kun 謝鯤 (fourth century): she knocked two of his teeth out with her weaving shuttle.[17] Su Shi advises his friend to seek out another of his acquaintances, an old woman who had said to Su, "Those days when you advised the emperor in the Hanlin Academy, haven't they vanished like a spring dream?" In honor of her philosophical attitude, people called her "Old Mother Spring Dream." Such company might help reconcile Old Fu to his failures in life.

Cow patties, wild scallions used as playground trumpets, the society of children, beggars, and has-beens: Su Shi stages his banishment to such settings with humor rather than bitterness. A similar self-derision colors this probably inauthentic poem:

野徑行行遇小童，黎音笑語說坡翁。
東行策杖尋黎老，打狗驚雞似病風。[18]

After walking long on the rustic path I meet a small boy
Who with Li accent and smiling manner addresses me as
    "Old Mr. Dongpo."
I continue eastward with my cane in search of the Li elders,
Smiting dogs and scattering chickens like a man deranged.

In a more elevated register, Su Shi portrayed an indigenous firewood gatherer in terms that recall one of the permanent figures of the Chinese literary tradition, the hermit free from all worldly ambition who mocks the disappointed scholar and treats the supposedly civilized being as someone to be pitied:

黎山有幽子，形槁神獨完。
負薪入城市，笑我儒衣冠。
生不聞詩書，豈知有孔顏。
翛然獨往來，榮辱未易關。
日暮鳥獸散，家在孤雲端。
問答了不同，歎息指屢彈。
似言君貴人，草莽栖龍鸞。
遺我古貝布，海風今歲寒。[19]

There is a solitary man on Mount Li,
Gaunt of body but unimpaired in spirit.
With a load of kindling on his back he enters the town
And laughs at my scholar's robe and cap.
Not once in his life has he heard of the *Odes* or the
    Documents;
How would he know the names of Confucius or Jia Yan?
With utter freedom he comes and goes.
Honor and dishonor mean nothing to him.
At day's end when birds and beasts scatter to their lairs,
His home is at the edge of a lonely cloud.
No conversation with him is possible;
I can do no more than sigh and flick my fingers.
He seems to say: "Sir, you are a noble being,
A dragon or phoenix come to nest in our grasses."
He offers me a piece of cotton-tree fabric,
For the sea wind is cold this year.

Su Shi, Old Mr. Dongpo, was determined to make the best of a bad situation. Though he expected his banishment to be indefinite, he was not willing to fall into the self-pity and isolation of certain of his eminent literary predecessors. The model for Su Shi's exile will not be the wronged Qu Yuan, constantly protesting his own righteousness, nor the grouchy Han Yu or Liu Zongyuan, seeking consolation in rocks and trees, but Tao Yuanming, who retired from official service and went to live in the country for his own peace of mind. In poems echoing Tao Yuanming's rhymes and emulating his manner, and inspired by politeness and gratitude toward his local hosts as well, Su Shi occasionally makes statements that verge on hyperbole. For example:

借我三畝地，結茅為子鄰。
欸舌倘可學，化為黎母民。[20]

If someone will lend me three acres of ground
I'll thatch a roof and make a house next to yours.

And if that shrike tongue of theirs can be learnt,
I'll transform into a child of Mother Li.

(The central mountain of Hainan, Mount Li, was considered the mother of all the island's indigenous inhabitants.) Did Su Shi actually envision himself "going native" and becoming a Li? Probably not; but the fact that he could imagine (even rhetorically) putting down roots in this way and turning his back on his literary reputation and the life of the capital is already a kind of Zhuangzian reversal of values. As Yang Zhiyi observes, Su Shi's readiness to "depict the periphery as morally superior to the center" is "unprecedented."[21]

As if to find himself a part to play in local life, Su Shi writes a series of poems echoing the rhymes of Tao Yuanming's "Quan nong." The preface observes:

海南多荒田，俗以貿香為業，所產秔稌不足於食，乃以藷芋雜米作粥糜以取飽。余既哀之，乃和淵明《勸農》詩，以告其有知者。[22]

In Hainan are many fields left fallow. The inhabitants sell aloeswood to get a living. The glutinous rice they grow is not enough for them to eat, so they resort to a mixture of taro and assorted grains to fill their bellies. Lamenting their plight, I followed the rhymes of [Tao] Yuanming's "Exhortations to the Tillers" to inform the more educated among the local people.

咨爾漢黎，均是一民。
鄙夷不訓，夫豈其真。
怨忿劫質，尋戈相因。
欺謾莫訴，曲自我人。 ...

Hearken, ye Han and Li! We are but one people.
"Disobedient, uncouth savages"—is this your true nature?
Feuds and resentment, robbery and hostage taking, cause
        one side after another to take weapons,
Trickery and imposture with none to do justice: the fault
        comes from my kind. . . .

天禍爾土，　不麥不稷。
民無用物，　怪珍是殖。
播厥熏木，　腐餘是稽。
貪夫汙吏，　鷹鷙狼食。

Heaven has sent down disaster on your land; it produces
neither barley nor millet.
The common folk lack a useful crop: it's a perverse treasure
you plant,
"Sowing" the smoke-trees and harvesting their rotten
remnants,
So that greedy men and filthy officials can snatch like
hawks and devour like wolves.

The "perversity" of this local agriculture lay partly in the natural
history of the aquilaria tree. It produces its most valuable resinous
wood, known as agarwood or aloeswood, when it has been infected
with a parasite. The people of Hainan were harvesting, then, not
mature grain and fruits for their own use, but the already rotten
stumps of dead trees. This valuable export commodity then exposed them to the rapacity of traders on the international market.

豈無良田，　膴膴平陸。 . . .
聽我苦言，　其福永久。
利爾粗耜，　好爾鄰偶。
斬艾蓬藋，　南東其畝。
父兄搰梃，　以抶游手。 . . .

Who can say that you lack good fields? You have level,
fertile ground. . . .
Hear my words of concern, offered to ensure your lasting
felicity.
Let your hoes be sharp and your neighborly relations warm.
Remove the weeds, extend your fields to the south and
east.
Let fathers and elder brothers wield the stick to beat the
idlers with. . . .

逸諺戲侮，博弈頑鄙。
投之生黎，俾勿冠履。
霜降稻實，千箱一軌。
大作爾社，一醉醇美。

Idlers, jokers, manipulators, gamblers, gamers, good-
for-nothings—
Drive them back among the wild Li, let them have neither
cap nor shoes.
When frost comes and your grain is ripe, with thousands
of baskets filled,
Grandly celebrate your Soil God festival in a haze of
mellow wine.

In his exhortations, Su Shi paraphrases the *Book of Documents*
and uses the four-character verse of the *Book of Songs*, as if to repeat the founding acts of Chinese culture on this exotic territory.
The much-quoted sentence about the identity of Han and Li occurs in the course of enacting this historical fiction. The poem is a
document of development policy, arguing for a reordering of the
economy of Hainan. The situation at the time of Su Shi's arrival is
this: Dealers from the mainland have been paying the Li to harvest
agarwood resin used in the production of luxury goods such as
incense and perfumes. The advantages of participating in this ex-
tractive industry, the greatest profits of which are certainly reserved to the exporters, have led the Li to neglect their fields. The
precontact agriculture based on taro demands little human input
and still provides a bare kind of sustenance for the aborigines who
exert themselves for the benefit of the incense traders. As has often
happened in human history, a commodity that is without value to
the people who live in an area but has great value for outsiders (e.g.,
oil, diamonds) is seized on by middlemen who do not have the
interests of the locals at heart. Claims over harvesting rights in the
incense tree groves are setting one group against another, seemingly disrupting the friendly relations of an earlier age. Su Shi
blames his own "kind" for this disorder and urges his hearers,

whether Han or Li, to band together against the unscrupulous traders and their allies among the island's officials. They should abandon the collecting of incense wood and put themselves to work tilling the soil. By growing grain, a form of agriculture that requires intensive human input, they will ensure their self-sufficiency for the future and, as a side benefit, repress idleness and bad behavior. The miscreants will be sent back to live among the "wild" or "unassimilated" Li (生黎), and the dutiful subjects will be progressively incorporated. The result, Su Shi promises, will be the founding of an archaic utopia around its altars of soil and grain, with harvest banquets and ale-brewing exactly as outlined in the *Records of Ritual*. This economy will support a stable hierarchy of roles in which fathers and elder brothers are the recognized leaders and—presumably—guarantee tax revenues for the prefectural government. Su Shi proposes the replacement of one model of development (commodity extraction for export) by another (intensive agriculture organized by family lineages, supporting local consumption and generating in-kind tax payments). This second pattern is the orthodox economic model of the agriculturally based Chinese dynastic states, from Shen Nong 神農, the Divine Husbandman (or whoever was the historical equivalent of that legendary personage) on down. Adopting this second pattern will require the Li to abandon their previous diet, calendar, and probably family organization and religious belief as well. (Su Shi's essay about the wasteful practice of cattle sacrifice, which the Li of Hainan performed in order to dispel contagious disease, suggests that religious habits and human sustenance are inseparable.[23]) So the writings of Su Shi on Hainan exhibit an openness to the non-Han or incompletely Sinicized people of the region, a sympathy for their difficulties, and a plan for their ever more complete integration into the Chinese world, in the guise of development. At least it is a more positive mode of development than the piratical extraction of surplus from natural resources that had predominated there.

Even when out of favor with the emperor, Su Shi seemingly cannot help acting on behalf of the empire. Today a kind of literary tourism commemorates Su Shi's residence on Hainan. Whether or not the Li followed Su's recommendations, the sinification of Hainan proceeded apace. One of the long-term effects of such sinification was to set up the necessary conditions for the education and distinguished career of Qiu Jun, the mandarin whose advice to the Ming emperor we were considering a few pages earlier as an example of the "civilizing mission" in particularly energetic form. Shifting to an economy based on grain cultivation, paying the taxes that resulted in more intensive administration, reorganizing people into patrilines, prioritizing the education of young men, identifying and rewarding talent—if these conditions had not been realized in a causal chain, there would have been no Qiu Jun. Although Qiu Jun, born on Hainan some 320 years after Su Shi's arrival, may appear to us as the archetypal Confucian mandarin with his philosophy of the top-down "transformation" of remote, alien, or alienated peoples into ideal subjects of the Way, his biography is that of a Hainanese who has perfectly assimilated and benefited from the codes of the meritocracy. Qiu Jun speaks with no discernible trace of his tropical origins: his authorial persona is one of unreserved identification with the center, with the "Great Learning" (*Da xue*) of which he is giving an "expanded elaboration" (*yanyi*).[24] He is an example of that whereof he speaks, a concrete illustration of "the looping effect of human kinds."[25]

Pamela Kyle Crossley, too, has discerned a kind of self-referential logic in the "Sinicization commonplace," the idea that outsiders who came into contact with Chinese would sooner or later adopt Chinese ways and be assimilated: "Its conceptual flaw lay in its circularity. To be 'Sinicized' was to become 'like the Chinese,' who were only those who had been previously sinicized. This is self-evidently counterhistorical in the sense that Chinese culture, the character of which is at issue in 'sinicization,' has been an uninterrupted process of mutation due in part to the challenging and differentiating effects of aboriginal, border and heterodox cultures."[26]

Rather than populations or cultures, we are here talking about the written record, and the difficulty of separating the idea of *hanhua* from the act of assimilating others comes to the fore in considering the language used to describe or address those others. Su Shi's means of representation implicitly drew the Li inhabitants of Hainan into the scenarios of the *Book of Documents*, the *Records of Ritual*, the poetry of Tao Qian, and so forth through allusion and metaphor. It is difficult to see how he could do otherwise, for the limits of his language, to borrow a saying from Wittgenstein, were the limits of his world; and that is true of all of us. If we apply a particularly stringent standard of respect for autonomy, an awareness of the performative effects of language, and a hermeneutic of suspicion, Su's friendly attitude toward his Hainan neighbors can be tagged as an act of colonization. Perhaps any description of their world in the Chinese language would lend weight to that assimilative process. Dismal tropics indeed, where to describe the Other, even as Other, is to make it the Same![27] Or would we prefer Han Yu's attitude of resignation to the impenetrability of "birdlike language and savage faces" 鳥言夷面? (Han Yu nonetheless managed to collect tax payments.) Su plainly thought that he was helping the Li with his energetic advocacy of the grain-based, lineage-based, tax-paying way of life, the best way of life he knew.

Might the intellectual heritage of China and its literary language allow for understanding outsiders without conquering or assimilating them? A test case is provided by the travel narrative of Changchun Zhenren 長春真人, "The Immortal of Everlasting Spring," no exile but an emissary traversing alien lands. His impressions of the Northwest in prose and verse, transcribed by his disciple Li Zhichang 李志常, were published under the title *Xiyouji* 西遊記 (not to be confused, of course, with the vastly more famous and later novel of the same name, *Xiyouji*, known as *Journey to the West*). Changchun Zhenren, an eminent Daoist master of the Quanzhen sect, was invited to offer counsel to Genghis Khan in the year 1220. Following pathways newly opened by Mongol conquests, he journeyed from Shandong to Beijing, through Mongolia, Samarkand, and on to the Hindu Kush in pursuit of the itinerant emperor's camp.[28] After passing through the Great Wall, he notes the ever more sparsely distributed houses and the ever wider plains, observing:

從此以西，漸有山阜，人煙頗眾，亦皆以黑車白帳爲家。其俗牧且獵，衣以韋毳，食以肉酪。男子結髮垂兩耳，婦人冠以樺皮…俗無文籍，或約之以言，或刻木爲契，遇食同享，難則爭赴，有命則不辭，有言則不易，有上古之遺風焉。以詩敘其實云：

極目山川無盡頭，風煙不斷水長流。
如何造物開天地？到此令人放馬牛。
飲血茹毛同上古，峨冠結髮異中州。
聖賢不得垂文化，歷代縱橫只自由。[29]

Going westward, one sees villages appear from time to time in the mountains, where the people are somewhat concentrated. They make their home in a black wagon covered with a white tent. They live from herding and hunting, dress in skins and furs, and feed on meat and yoghurt. The men wear their hair in two long braids behind the ears; the women wear a tall birch bark headdress. . . . They have no custom of writing. They make contracts either verbally or with an exchange of notched sticks. If they have food, everyone joins in; if anyone is in dire straits, all pitch in to help. They never disobey an order, never break a promise. Such were the customs of Antiquity. [The Immortal of Everlasting Spring] wrote a poem to commemorate these facts:

Mountains and rivers stretch out limitlessly;
Unceasing wind and fog, waters without end.
How did the Creator make this terrain productive?
By causing the people to raise horses and sheep.
They consume blood and flesh just as the first men did,
Coiffures and braids like theirs are not seen in the Central
　　States.
No need for the Sages to reveal Civilization to them:
From age to age, everywhere, only freedom has been
　　their lot.

I am not completely happy with the word "freedom" as translation of *ziyou* 自由 in this context, because it has been overlaid by so many modern meanings, especially the political ones. To get a better sense of what it is doing here, look at its placement in the lines, symmetrical and opposite to *wenhua* 文化, "civilization": *ziyou* here means a lack of constraining structures. As if to say: under normal conditions, the more *wenhua* you have, the less *ziyou*, and vice versa. These nomads realize the almost unthinkable condition of everyone fending for him- or herself and yet not becoming entangled in perpetual conflict.

The Daoist envoy combines observations with value judgments in his short description of the cross-border population. These nomads, encountered somewhere near the present Ulaanbaatar, fall in line with already ancient stereotypes of primitive man. They feed, dress, and house themselves with animal products, they do not cultivate the earth, and thus they correspond to a stage in Chinese history that must be sought in the far distant past, before even the age of Shen Nong, founder of agriculture. As one leaves Beijing and travels northwest, one travels backward in time. The nomads' ignorance of writing puts them outside the whole process of Chinese history, always heavily reliant on written memory: oracle bones, bronzes, bamboo slips, silk, paper, and so forth. This lack is not necessarily a failing. Having no means to deceive, they say yes when they mean yes, no when they mean no, and both good and bad fortune are communal, not private. Their customs are admirable though primitive; these are good, indeed noble, savages. An echo, or so it seems to me, of the Xianbei song about the sublime steppe landscape, its infinities of sky, highlands, and water, gives the savages' nobility an appropriately elevated backdrop.

Changchun Zhenren's positive impressions of these briefly encountered nomad groups put him in the intellectual lineage of Sima Qian, whose "Xiongnu liezhuan" 匈奴列傳, chapter 110 of the *Shiji* (*Records of the Grand Historian*), "effectively started an ethnography and a literate history of the north that also served as a model for later dynastic histories," a "master narrative" about the nomad lifestyle with incalculable subsequent influence on historiography and policy.[30] Nicola Di Cosmo sees two facets in Sima Qian's account of the northern peoples: one, a rich empirical documentation derived from firsthand interviews with people who had lived in the North and dealt with the Xiongnu; and two, a speculative and ideological response to the intellectual currents of the time. Sima Qian sought not only to record what had happened in history but to explain it; thus his empirical information contributes to a theory of the barbarian. This theory reposes on one constant: change. Pressed by the constant need to find new grazing areas and sources of water, the nomads create for themselves minimally constraining institutions that can be built and unbuilt moment by moment, contrasting with the Chinese empire's zeal for permanence and solidity and, above all, with the burden of laws, taxes, relationships, and obligations that determine every Chinese citizen's every move. If Sima Qian's contemporaries suspected him of "barbarophilia,"[31] the scheme of values that makes him see in barbarism a possible way of life stems from Laozi and the early Daoist school, which excelled, as Sima Qian's father Sima Tan put it, in "changing with the times and responding to the alterations of things" 與時遷移, 應物變化.[32] Nomads are always responding to change—by moving on. Though identifications of doctrine across fifteen hundred years are inherently dubious, it appears that with Changchun Zhenren it is once again someone claiming the heritage of Laozi who can see the outsiders as people worth emulating. The Mongol khan's invitation may also have prepared this Daoist to look favorably on the customs of the steppe. At least Changchun Zhenren shows no inclination to indoctrinate these nomads or convert their pastures into wheat fields.

Some five hundred years after the venerable Daoist passed through Ulaanbaatar and Samarkand on his way to converse with Genghis Khan about the mysteries of the universe, such *ziyou* was no longer available. The Qing emperors, when they looked northwest, saw territory to be put to use and populations to be removed or incorporated. Under Kangxi and Qianlong, they brought the

Northwest under their control. The Zunghar nation (a confederation of junior Mongol lineages, led by nobles outside the line of descent from Genghis Khan), showed too little subordination to the Qing and after fifteen years of off-and-on war were practically exterminated.[33] New outposts were built in the former Zunghar territory and surrounded with military colonies (*bingtun* 兵屯), penal colonies (*qiantun* 遣屯), and agricultural colonies (*hutun* 戶屯). Along with soldiers, administrators, internal migrants, and the merchants who arrived to supply the above-mentioned groups, those outposts also housed a number of disgraced officials, sent there to live out their terms of exile.

One such was Ji Yun 紀昀, chief editor of the massive *Siku quanshu* 四庫全書 and a Hanlin scholar renowned for his wit and learning but not careful enough in his personal dealings. Working at the very summit of Qing officialdom, Ji Yun came to have advance knowledge of a bribery investigation that involved his son-in-law. For divulging this privileged information, Ji was sentenced to two years' banishment to Ürümqi in Xinjiang. While there, Ji kept a notebook, and after his return he reorganized his notes into a collection of 160 four-line poems, *Wulumuqi zashi* 烏魯木齊雜詩 (Occasional poems from Ürümqi).[34] Perhaps on account of their being composed after his period of exile had been completed and Ji Yun was back in the emperor's good graces, the poems, as one contemporary observed, are free of bitterness and protest.[35] They are, rather, the record of a curious observer, alert to new features of landscape, climate, and custom and eager to document the changes that Qing resettlement was bringing to the region. The effect is (to put it anachronistically) similar to a photo album: snapshots selected from local life and framed by the narrative of a journey. What any traveler notices is, of course, what that person is prepared to notice; what is written down is what is deemed worthy of the reader's curiosity. A shared context of prior information prepares reader and writer to see and respond together. Every poem in the collection deals in familiarity and surprise, two dimensions constantly in play.

The series opens:

山圍芳草翠烟平， 迢遞新城接舊城。
行到叢祠歌舞榭， 綠氍毹上看棋枰。[36]

Mountains edge a plain of fresh grass and emerald haze:
In the distance, the new city added to the old.
Ascending to the forest shrine, one can hear song and
    dance from the stage
And observe the checkerboard pattern of green fields.

Ji Yun's notes observe that the old town was situated too far
from sources of water, and the new one, named Dihua 迪化 or
"Conveying Transformation," is better located. North of the city
is a hill crowned with a temple of Guandi, from which one can
observe the layout of theaters and city walls. He opens, then, with
what Hollywood would call an "establishing shot."

The seasons are not the same as in North-Central China:

山田龍口引泉澆， 泉水惟憑積雪消。
頭白藩王年八十， 不知春雨長禾苗。 (2)

The mountain fields are irrigated by water piped from a
    fountain,
This fountain water being nothing but accumulated
    snowmelt.
A white-headed local has never heard in all his eighty years
Of spring rains that cause the rice sprouts to grow.

"Good land is easy to find; water is hard to get" 良田易得水難
求 (26). The economy of the region had been transformed since
1756 by the implantation of Chinese agricultural colonies. Soils left
fallow or used as pasture for millennia, now irrigated by the snows
of the Tianshan range, produced wheat so abundantly that it sold
for less than it cost to produce it, an unheard-of development in an
age when scarcity was the rule. The price of grain was not the only
anomaly noted by Ji Yun. The imbalance of men and women in the
military and settler population replaced the custom of the bride's

family giving a dowry with the man's family giving a bride price: an almost cosmological reversal. The phrase "shei zhi" 誰知 ("who would have thought it?") appears often in the collection to mark these moments of astonishment at the wonders and paradoxes of the Far West. Each instance of reversal recalls the customs of the capital and the long-settled central regions as the norm. Ways of life that depart from the norm are noteworthy. Some of them have already been discovered by wily entrepreneurs and arbitrageurs (and Ji Yun, publishing his poetry collection, may be one such).

The inhabitants of the Far West drink heavily: dealers in wine and spirits go back East every year with twenty or thirty taels of profit from supporting this habit (poem 35, note).

Smoking from water pipes astonishes our narrator:

冉冉春雲出手邊，逢人開篋不論錢。
火神一殿千金直，檀越誰知是水煙。(7)

Fluffy spring clouds rise close at hand.
On meeting a friend, the tobacco case opens, no talk of
　　money!
The Fire God has his temple worth a thousand in gold.
Its benefactor—who would have thought it?—is named
　　"Water and Smoke."

(Ji Yun's note: "The Western people have the habit of smoking from a hookah. Loafers always have their tobacco pouch at the ready, and when they encounter a friend, they invite him to smoke with no thought of repayment; instead, the smoker goes and makes an offering to the Fire God. In this way this god has become master of a temple worth a thousand in gold. A temple built on nothing but smoke and water!")

The dogs of the Northwest impose themselves on the newcomer's attention:

麗譙未用夜誰何，寒犬霜牙利似磨。
只怪深更齊吠影，不容好夢到南柯。(10)

No need for watchtowers or the challenge, "Who goes
    there?"
The frost-white teeth of these northern dogs are whetstone
    sharp.
But when they bark at shadows in the middle of the night
The dreamer can never attain his Southern Branch. [37]

The region's economic development attracts peddlers and dealers of all kinds. There are shadowy Tibetans:

吐蕃部落久相親，賣果時時到市闤。
恰似春深梁上燕，自來自去不關人。(12)

The Tibetan tribesmen keep to themselves,
Coming from time to time to sell nuts in the city market.
Exactly like the late-spring swallows in the rafters,
They come and go, heedless of human beings.

(The silent-footed aboriginal is a constant in travel literature.) Or
there are Mongols engaged in the traditional exchange of horses
for bricks of tea:

敕勒陰山雪乍開，騣汗隊隊過龍堆。
殷勤譯長稽名字，不比尋常估客來。(12)

When the snow begins to melt on Mount Yin in the Chi-le
    territory,
Long-haired ponies pass in small groups through Longdui.
The head translator checks the names and surnames
    carefully,
For these are not the usual kind of merchant.

(The Mongolian horse trade was limited to holders of a state license, hence the extra attention.)
    Ji Yun was familiar with the inherited tradition of frontier po-
etry: note, for example, the echo of the Xianbei "Chi-le song" from
the *Yuefu shiji*, with its opening words 敕勒川，陰山下. That tradition, in fact, allows Ji Yun to write in a generous and free manner

befitting his subject, as Qian Daxin observes in his preface to the work: 無郁輴愁苦之音, 而有春容渾脱之趣, "it lacks the melancholy or bitter tone [of much exile poetry] and makes an inclusive, generous-minded impression." Borders are here shown as being transcended and cultural barriers removed. Ji Yun and his fellow exiles can enjoy wines, vegetables, and even fish from the central regions of China thanks to the commercial ties reaching up into the Northwest. Music and theater in Ürümqi are in no way inferior to those of the capital. Ji Yun's journey to Xinjiang attests to the transformative power of the Qing dynasty at the moment of its greatest expansion. As a chronicler of cultural diffusion, Ji Yun points to evidence of the ritual order of the Central States now visible in the far Northwest:

金碧觚棱映翠嵐, 崔嵬紫殿往東南。
時時一曲昇平樂, 膜拜聞呼萬歲三。(5)

Gold, jade, profiles of ritual vases standing out amid
    greenish smoke:
To a purple temple atop a mountain peak we proceeded
    southeast.
From time to time the air "Shengping" starts up again
And everyone kotows to the thrice-repeated call of "Ten
    thousand years!"

(Ji Yun's note: "The ceremony of congratulations to the court is held at the Wanshougong temple, southeast of town. Music, assembly of officials, exactly as in the central regions. Representatives of the military and administration as well as merchants put on shows as signs of gratitude. Local people perform their offerings sincerely and without skimping. The same thing happens at Ku'erkelawusu [庫爾喀喇烏蘇].")

Not only culture but nature is modified by the arrival of people from the Central Regions. Ji Yun writes, "Ten thousand hearth fires have warmed the clouds / And melted the ancient snows of the Tianshan range" 萬家煙火暖雲蒸, 鎖盡天山太古冰 (1). In a note he adds: "The climate here has always been extremely cold, but in the past few years it has begun to resemble that of the Inner Regions" 向來氣候極寒，數載以來漸同內地人氣盛也.

As a final and complete sign of normalization, the local administration declares the opening of civil service examinations in Ürümqi:

山城是處有弦歌，錦帙牙簽市上多。
為報當年鄭漁仲，儒書今過斡難河。(11)

It's a mountain fortress, but within it string music and song
    can be heard.
The markets are full of embroidered book covers and ivory
    clasps.
As if to respond to old Zheng Qiao,
Confucian books have finally passed the River Wonan!

(Ji Yun's note: "Zheng Qiao 鄭樵 had said in [his phonological treatise] *Qi Yin lüe* 七音略 that the books of Confucius would never go a single step beyond the River Wonan / Onon [which runs north of the present Mongolian/Russian frontier]. Up to now, there were no booksellers beyond the pass. One might occasionally find romances and tales of the supernatural mixed up with other goods for sale by northwestern peddlers. But now that a cohort of examination candidates has been fixed, shops specializing in books have opened.")

Contact with alien cultures is much less significant to Ji Yun than the arrival of the culture that he recognizes as his own. I have not done a quantitative analysis of the themes of this collection of 160 poems, but it is clear that whether he speaks of landscapes, weather, old ruins, feast days, melons, mushrooms, forests, snakes, iron implements, medicines, camels, flowers, oranges, fish, tobacco, horses, ducks, almonds, coal, ghosts, or other images of the faraway country, Ji Yun never enters into conversation with an inhabitant of Xinjiang or inquires into his thoughts and wishes. It is not just that Ji Yun congratulates Xinjiang on having acquired some of the symbols of assimilation to the Chinese way of life: according to his poetry at least, he spends his time in exile among other former Pekingese, eating and entertaining himself exactly as at home. *Wulumuqi zashi* is not really a work of ethnography, if by ethnography we understand the description of cultural others and the effort to understand them. Rather, it is an auto-ethnography of the colony of transplanted Chinese residing in Xinjiang, an account of rapid change and the development of a new society, an enclave that is causing a certain hybridization of the society around it through contact with its edges. The enthusiastic reception the book met with at the time must be at least partly due to the way it imagines Xinjiang as an infusion of Chinese culture into a foreign landscape, and not to any great degree as a clash of Chinese culture with an unyielding foreign culture. It tells us that cultural expansion still works, even in the Northwest. One message that can be taken from this cheerful book is that there really is no such thing as banishment anymore. A person can be held at a distance from the capital, but no longer will exotic figures with shrike-like tongues and tattooed bodies make him doubt his place in the world.

Between his return from exile and the writing of *Wulumuqi zashi*, Ji Yun received an imperial commission to compose an ode on the return of the Torghuts, a junior Mongol lineage that had resided in Russia for 150 years and recently chosen to seek readmission to China.[38] The Qing welcomed them and settled them on the territories formerly occupied by the Zunghars, considered disloyal. In his ode written for the Qianlong emperor's ceremony of welcome to the Torghut leaders, Ji Yun presented the return of the Torghuts as a confirmation of the theory once expressed by Mencius, that a true king is one who attracts distant peoples by the merits of his rule. "Such being indeed the case," said Mencius, "the people must flock to him, as water flows downwards with a rush, which no one can repress" 誠如是也，民歸之，由水之就下，沛然誰能禦之.[39] Ji Yun's rendition of the theme is hyperbolic:

釀化超三古，　元功被八紘。
聖朝能格遠，　絕域盡輸誠。

Benevolent rule exceeding that of the Three Patriarchs!
A mighty achievement covering the entire world!
Our August Dynasty is able to draw near those who are far,
Extending to the remotest regions its sincerity.

益地圖新啟，　鈞天樂正鳴，
殽蒸雕俎列，　酒醴羽觴盈。

A vaster land now opens for [the Torghuts] to cultivate,
Happiness resounds from all quarters.
Exquisite provisions are laid out,
Wine stands ready in winged vessels.

帶礪崇封錫，　衣冠異數榮。
試看歌舞樂，　真覺畏懷並。

Belt with whetstone, badges of office,
Caps and gowns of countless types, all bedazzle.
Taste the delights of song and dance:
Enlightenment and awe arise together!

從此皇風暢，　彌彰帝道亨。
梯航遍陬澨，　寅臚集寰瀛。[40]

Henceforth let the imperial spirit flow unrestricted!
Let the royal way be fully realized!
Let travelers explore all corners of the world,
Departing to the whole of land and sea.

What Ji Yun is here imagining is a literal realization of the dream of universal sovereignty in ancient texts: "Wherever human steps can go, wherever ships and oars can reach, no place is outside its jurisdiction"人跡所至，舟楫所通，莫不為郡縣.[41] We might call this centralizing cosmopolitanism: the ambition to cover the entire world with a civilization that is imperial, Confucian, and native to the Central States. That civilization is self-evidently a matter of rule, but also of language, writing, and ideology. There is no essential limit to its expansion, as can be seen from its spread to areas far outside the Central States, where different languages were displaced, extinguished, or overlaid by the Chinese character. It does, however, run up against empirical limits to expansion, as marked by differences in script: despite Ji Yun's confident prophecies, the Northwest and Southeast have never entirely been painted over by the culture of the center. In this sense, the vocation of Chinese literature to be a world literature is coeval with the universalistic tendency of Chinese political philosophy and the state expansions for which it provided intellectual justification.

In previous chapters I've recalled that this expansion, when it has occurred in the past, has usually been at the expense of other languages, polities, and cultures. Is this the natural tendency of what we call Chinese culture? Or has expansion been a repeated moment in a fluctuating balance between purity and hybridity, monolingualism and polyglottism, the deciding factors of which lie not in Chinese culture itself but in its shifting power relations with its Others? I return to the notion of the same boundary looking quite different from its two sides. A person on the Chinese side of the boundary can approach it in a monolingual, monocultural, ahistorical way: "the Tabgach," he or she may say, "have always been one of the ethnic minorities of our country." A Tabgach observer, or anyone approaching from the other side of the boundary, is apt to have a different memory of what happened in the past, who was who, and what this means about group membership in the present.

We who read, love, and profess Chinese literature must resist the temptation to frame it as an infinitely expanding monoculture. Some of our familiar moves toward acknowledging pluralism in Chinese cultural history—the ritual inclusion of "national minorities," the "sinicization" thesis, and the notion of the nonexclusive coexistence of the "Three Teachings"—may be better described as gestures designed to absorb dissent and keep the intellectual momentum on the Huaxia side of the boundary. But as Zhuang

Zhou observed long ago, "Considered from the side of their differences [*yi* 異], liver and gall are as far apart as Chu and Yue; considered from the side of their sameness [*tong* 同], all things are just one thing" 自其異者視之, 肝膽楚越也; 自其同者視之, 萬物皆一也.[42] There is a benefit to considering the differences (異) between Chu, Yue, and all the other components of Chinese civilization. The undeniable force of acculturation operating over so many centuries should not mask the mutual adjustment, the transculturation, that cannot occur unless languages, writings, and cultural systems disagree in some irreducible way. Our exiles encountered that difference, though most of them felt compelled to do something about it—which, for exponents of literate culture, meant overcoming it with sameness (同). Which is understandable, considering that they were sent to experience difference as a punishment.

Conclusion

Frames, Edges, Escape Codes

宕然喪其天下焉

JI YUN'S EXPERIENCES of exile—personal and vicarious—only confirmed his attachment to the center. Rejoicing to see Peking opera and examination textbooks arrive in the Xinjiang oases, exulting in the Torghuts' return from Russian durance, he versified in various forms the incorporation of the margins into the center, the principle of imperial "centrality and commonality." As far as Ji Yun could know (he died in 1805), the process of expansion had not come anywhere near its limits. Xinjiang was a live frontier. The Qing would continue to claim, lose, and reclaim new territories in Central Asia until the 1880s.[1] During those years, a new front of foreign troubles opened on the southeast coast, as British and French fleets extorted concessions and moved northward. As a result, the primary referent of the word *xi* 西 ("the West") in Chinese swerved from being the arid territories where the Silk Road once ran to being the lands where ladies wore hoop skirts, cheese was eaten, and the art of mechanized killing progressed most rapidly. One of Ji Yun's successors in Xinjiang exile was Lin Zexu 林則徐, the imperial commissioner who had attempted to bring the British opium merchants under the law.

Between Ji Yun and Lin Zexu runs a boundary. It is the boundary between a triumphant and a defensive China, between China as center and China as margin, between a China that cared little for translations and one that depended anxiously on them.

Ji Yun's world was packed with cultural and linguistic difference. But that diversity had no value to him—it was diversity in the sense of not yet being assimilated. And the world that Lin Zexu was one of the first in China to ascertain was organized around cultural and linguistic differences of another kind. The task of recovering a multilingual premodern Asia involves chipping away at two totalizing world pictures: the familiar one of East-West polarity, and the older one of Chinese imperial centrality.[2]

———

The goal of comparative study, it seems to me, is finding counterexamples, edges and bits of texture that fall somewhat out of frame. They enable us to see the frame as a frame. They are escape codes that get us out of the "Full Screen" attention economy of a world picture. Thanks to them, no world picture can ever be enough.

"One curious thing about the ontological problem," W. V. O. Quine once said snappily, "is its simplicity." It holds in three short words: "What is there?"[3] I would add that only one more word is needed to state the comparative problem: "What else is there?"

What is there? Primarily and obviously, there is a world order or a world picture. For those who live in it, is *the* world. Fine; what else is there?

"What else?"—that is, what exceptions, what trespasses, what areas not covered by any category, what wildernesses or shadows beyond the horizon of present vision? We cannot know anything unless we know what it is not (an insight voiced by Spinoza and Saussure, among others).[4] "What is China?"—a question many have asked. If it is permitted to answer a question with a question, I would suggest asking, "China, as opposed to what?" In other words, what China has been or how it has been variously realized is certainly part of the answer, but another indispensable part will involve what it has not been: a catalog that must include nomadic-pastoral peoples, Miao, Yi, Tibetans, Uyghurs, Mongols, Japanese, kings of Goguryeo, and the like, who for one reason or another could not be considered Chinese. Their specific ways of not being Chinese are each part of the perimeter of Chinese civilization. So are the expedients whereby the representatives of that civilization have variously excluded, included, subordinated, or assimilated them.

The capacity to create and live among works of literature has long been central to Chinese self-understanding. The "civilizing process" separates, to use the traditional vocabulary, into facets of *wen* 文 and *wu* 武, the arts of governance and spiritual cultivation on the inside and the techniques of war on the outside. Being sited on a border, translation participates in both of those correlated registers of identity management. Since they involve, by definition, the subordination of alien peoples, empires demand translation, but most frequently they use it and forget it. Translations permit the assimilation of what will become imperial cultural heritage and leave on the other side of the border what will be considered "barbarian." Civilizations each manufacture their own barbarians.[5]

One of the ironies of comparative literary history at the scale I am proposing here is that a genre extolled as indispensable to the founding of civilization in one cultural system represents unassimilable barbarism in another. I return, for diagnostic purposes, to the "epic question." The heroic verse epic, a form of verbal art that surrounds China on three sides but awakened little or no interest within it, is one sign that tells us where the non-Chinese culture zone begins.[6] No ancient Greek could imagine that Homer would count as barbaric: it was rather the lack of familiarity with Homer that defined the *barbaroi*. Nonrecognition of this kind marks a sharp border. Not much hybridity can be expected to occur across such a wall. But subtler regional and temporal distinctions allow for livelier interchanges and variants. With their dependence on functional analysis of constituents of language, on the one hand, and their analogy to the aural patternings of music, on the other, verse forms mark and cross borders— borders that do not necessarily coincide with national or linguistic ones. Another premodern cosmopolitan literary region could be drawn from the occurrence of types of long-form fiction (a question muddled by teleologies of the "rise of the novel," which too often relegate *xiaoshuo, monogatari,* and the like to the unrewarding role of "precursors").[7] Other literary isoglosses must await discovery.[8] It is an advance in the understanding of culture to be able to draw as closely as possible the exact lines across which historical Dorothys have transited and paused to say, "Toto, I have a feeling we're not in Kansas anymore." Or those across which historical Sternes have gazed and pronounced: "They order, said I, this matter better in France."[9]

Like any universalizing civilization, Chinese civilization is reluctant to define its limits from the inside. Contact with incomprehensible languages, unrecognizable letters, unacceptable customs, and disloyal vassals is necessary to reveal them. Translation and cultural mediation are often called on to smooth the edges. Failures to translate—whether absence of translations, nontranslations, or unsuccessful translations—instruct us about boundaries; they break the frame. And even the Chinese literary code, with its infinite subtlety and vast resources, has limits; it is important to find these. So in these pages the translations that have mediated between the China of the time and what was not China, and often mediated non-China right into China, have been the object of our attention. Translation, of course, is not the whole story: the practices of cultural supremacy include as well such actions as migration, conquest, policy making, censorship, name changing, and the creation of specious knowledge.

While tracing the spatial and temporal boundaries of Chinese civilization, we were also reminded of the limits of other proposed world systems. To generalize somewhat, exclusionary concepts with a basis in teleologies of group identity create, or worse, motivate zones of ignorance or monolingualism. The word "world" often denotes, misleadingly, an area surrounded by such zones—zones of obscurity or mystery, if you will. The people in a world may cooperate in its boundary construction and maintenance. An invisible barrier, because unacknowledged, is more effective than a wall that all can see (even, as legend has it, from the moon).

Not everyone in a world accepts its totality. There will always be inquisitive or temperamentally metaphysical subjects who cannot agree that "the limits of my language are the limits of my world."[10] Thus the picture of worlding I have just drawn may strike some as overly cynical. But at least it takes the problem of horizons seriously.

It is the reward of comparison, but also its first step, to be able to chart such horizons and propose alternatives to self-evident truths.

Practitioners of literary comparison used to sort themselves into separate tribes: the historicists and the typologists. Historicists searched for demonstrable textual links—signs of influence—between authors and works. (Does Proust mention Dostoevsky? If so, how did he become aware of the earlier author?) Typologists looked for similarities between authors and works, regardless of era, language, and attested influences (can *À la recherche du temps perdu* and *Honglou meng* 紅樓夢 [*Dream of the Red Chamber*] be subordinated to a wider category of "the autobiographical novel"?).[11] Both practices break frames: they show that the author is not a self-contained, autonomous source of meaning, that any work is at least partially built out of other works, that no national literary tradition is an island. And the effects are (I think) wholly salutary. Some may worry that typological comparison across cultural units leads to a fatuous universalism ("and so we see that Man everywhere has been led to discover Truths and create works of Beauty"). If the polemic with self-contained models of culture is kept up, it can be less fatuous.

By showing the often conflicted, always changing, sometimes submerged history of relations between Chinese culture and those on its borders, we dissolve several existing frames and open up a field of investigation. This book has mainly worked the border—it has beat the bounds—from the inside, from within the traditions conveyed in the Chinese written language, but a complementary and much larger study would explore the other sides of the perimeter in their own terms, and the terms they set for their dialogue with their own outsides: Asian literary history as an interrelated "world."[12] "World literature" does not begin with Goethe, does not necessarily assimilate outlying territories into a European norm, does not lead to "us." Exploring worlds of literary art, for example (but only for example) in Asia, over the whole history of recorded culture gives us more than a few opportunities to break frames.[13]

———

Zoom, a wordless picture book, leads us through a series of perceptions and framings.[14] A coral-red surface with speckles and scalloped edges proves, when the page is turned, to have been the comb of a rooster being inspected by two children leaning on a windowsill. The children, at the turning of the next page, are in a farmhouse, which (turn the page) sits in a field amid bits of wall and cars. But inexplicably huge fingers dangle over part of that field: turn the page and the mystery is resolved—the farm is a toy farm and a bored-looking girl is setting pieces into it. Why are there big fragments of letters in the top left-hand corner? Because the girl is only a photograph on the cover of a toy catalog, which, with another turn of the page, we discover to be hanging from the listless hands of a boy sitting on a porch chair on the deck of a cruise ship, which, two or three more turns of the page inform us, is an image in an advertisement affixed to the side of a New York city bus in traffic, which (page turn) a Navajo elder is observing on a small television, which scene (page turn) figures on a stamp on an envelope, which. . . . With each reframing (or, as we say in my profession, "contextualization"), we observers step into a slightly larger reality that includes the preceding reality only to disavow it as a mere representation of a reality, which is exactly what will happen to the frame we are currently accepting as reality as soon as we turn the next page. Readers attentive to their own mental states can feel the click and switch between reality and representation, between empathy and objectification, whether they choose to flip the pages forward or backward. As long as nesting and unnesting of contexts is possible, comparison (before/after, inside/outside, real/unreal) can occur. A context is a relay from one context to another, well beyond the number nine fixed by the early documents of Chinese diplomatic translation. *Zoom* ends with a starry sky seen from space, and Earth an indistinguishable dot: the ultimate context? On reaching that page, we are definitely seeing all things as one, and not comparing anymore.

ACKNOWLEDGMENTS

THIS BOOK BEGAN as a series of lectures delivered on the invitation of the Center for Chinese Cultural Subjectivity, National Chengchi University, Taipei, Taiwan. I am grateful to the Center's director, Professor Lin Yuan-tse 林遠澤, and to Professor Kang Chan 詹康 for their friendly welcome. For good cheer and intellectual accompaniment through the writing and rewriting process I particularly thank Héctor Castaño, Kai Marchal, and Wen-jun Huang 黃雯君, also of the Center. Probing questions asked by Kevin Chang 張谷銘, David Holm, Siao-chen Hu 胡曉真, Sebastian Hsien-hao Liao 廖咸浩, Lin Hsiu-ling 林秀玲, Dinu Luca, and Song Chia-fu 宋家復 made me think harder (though surely not hard enough!). As the manuscript developed, part or all of it benefited from the careful reading of Kang-i Sun Chang, Timothy Billings, Romain Graziani, Andrew Hui, Dinu Luca, Elvin Meng, Casey Schoenberger, and Jonathan Stalling. Conversations with Anne Cheng, Shadi Bartsch-Zimmer, Christopher Bush, Stéphane Feuillas, Eric Hayot, Masato Hasegawa, Mikhail Khodorkovsky, Lucas Klein, Ulrich Timme Kragh, Sangjin Park, Dagmar Schäfer, and Martin Svensson Ekström, among others, helped it take shape. Dai Lianbin 戴聯斌 and Zhang Yan 張豔 caught mistakes and suggested improvements. Years ago, team teaching with Timothy Brook, Bob Batchelor, Roger Hart, and Charles Egan at Stanford first led me to wonder about the histories yet to be written of different modes of Chinese identity. For bibliographic help, I am grateful to Zhou Yuan and Jiaxun Benjamin Wu of the University of Chicago Libraries.

I wish to thank the two anonymous readers for the press, especially reader 2, whose commitment to getting things right saved me from numerous blunders and whose measured appreciation of the first draft made me all the more determined to improve it. I am grateful to Anne Savarese for her interest in the project and Anita O'Brien for her meticulous copyediting.

None of these kind people, of course, should be held responsible for my errors.

The International Comparative Literature Association, during the terms of three of its presidents (Hans Bertens, Zhang Longxi, and Sandra Bermann), has given impetus to the project of a literary history of East Asia from a comparative point of view. I am grateful for the confidence they have placed in me and for the opportunity to discuss plans for the history at ICLA-AILC meetings. The Neubauer Collegium of the University of Chicago has supported gatherings contributing to this project, as has the American Council of Learned Societies. I am especially thankful to Yang Qu and He Yanxiao for co-organizing two of these meetings. Another Neubauer Collegium project, which brought together Judith Farquhar, Ge Zhaoguang, Liu Dong, Xie Shaobo, Wang Min'an, and me for a month in each of three years to discuss historiography, guided my thinking about related questions; I hope that the results of those meetings will soon appear in print.

Parts of the research that went into the book were conducted at the American Academy in Berlin and the Max Planck Institute for the History of Science. The Humanities Division of the University of Chicago has been generous to me in many ways.

Most of all, I am grateful to Olga Viktorovna Solovieva for daily conversation, inspiration, and partnership. She, René, Constantin, Kirill, and Mila have been the best of companions.

H. S.
Chicago, April 2021

NOTES

Introduction

1. "Zhong" is not the only Chinese term for the Chinese. Others to be encountered in this study, with varying connotations, are Hua 華 ("flowering, flourishing"), Xia 夏 ("great" or "wide," also the name of an ancient dynasty), Zhuxia 諸夏 ("the many Xia"), and Huaxia 華夏 ("the flourishing Xia"). And let it be said explicitly that the content of the "center" or *zhong* has undergone countless changes over the centuries, as rival factions contended for that position and successive forces displaced it. But those modifications are not the main object of this book.

2. *Li ji* 禮記 [Records of ritual], "Zhongyong" 中庸, sec. 28, in *Shisan jing zhushu* 十三經注疏, ed. Ruan Yuan 阮元 (1815; reprint, Taipei: Dahua, 1987), 5:3544: compare the translation by James Legge, *The Doctrine of the Mean*, in *The Chinese Classics* (reprint, Taipei: SMC, 1991), 1:424. On this passage and its echoes elsewhere, see chapter 2 below.

3. Sima Qian 司馬遷, chap. 123 ("Da Yuan zhuan" 大宛傳) of *Shiji* 史記, 10 vols. (Beijing: Zhonghua shuju, 1959), 10:3166.

4. Burton Watson, trans., Sima Qian, *Records of the Grand Historian: Han Dynasty*, 2 vols. (New York: Columbia University Press, 1993), 2:236. The ethnonyms are somewhat conjectural. I have replaced Watson's paraphrase, "who would come translating and retranslating their languages," with the more literal "and languages requiring ninefold translation." On Sima Qian's rendition of the Central Asian geography of Zhang Qian, see Tamara T. Chin, *Savage Exchange: Han Imperialism, Chinese Literary Style, and the Economic Imagination* (Cambridge, MA: Harvard University Asia Center, 2014), 170–82.

5. The phrase *juli de zuzhi* 距離的組織 is the title of a poem by Bian Zhilin 卞之琳; for a thoughtful analysis, see Lucas Klein, *The Organization of Distance: Poetry, Translation, Chineseness* (Leiden: Brill, 2018), 25–44.

6. As James Legge long ago surmised, "China [or *Zhongguo* 中國, the Central State(s)] is evidently so denominated from its being thought to be surrounded by barbarous tribes" (*The Chinese Classics*, 1:379). For a perspective on centrality

contrasting somewhat with that presented here, see Tu Wei-ming, *Centrality and Commonality: An Essay on Confucian Religiousness* (Albany: State University of New York Press, 1989). On the ellipse with its two foci as a suggestive geometrical model for comparative study, see David Damrosch, "World Literature Today," *Symploke* 8 (2000): 7–19.

7. Johann Peter Eckermann, *Gespräche mit Goethe in den letzten Jahren seines Lebens 1823–1832* (Leipzig: Brockhaus, 1837), 325, as translated in *The Princeton Sourcebook in Comparative Literature*, ed. David Damrosch, Natalie Melas, and Mbongiseni Buthelezi (Princeton, NJ: Princeton University Press, 2009), 22. On Goethe's Chinese readings, see Heinrich Detering and Yuan Tan, *Goethe und die chinesischen Fräulein* (Göttingen: Wallstein, 2018); and César Domínguez, "In 1837/1838: World Literature and Law," *Critical Inquiry* 47, no. 1 (2020): 28–48.

8. Karl Marx and Friedrich Engels, "Manifesto of the Communist Party," in *Selected Works in One Volume* (New York: International Publishers, 1968), 36.

9. An influential presentation of this analysis is Immanuel Wallerstein, *The Modern World-System*, 3 vols. (New York: Academic Press, 1976–1989).

10. George Woodberry, "Editorial," *Journal of Comparative Literature* 1 (1903): 3–4. On Woodberry's journal and its reception, see Ivan Lupić, "English and Comparative Literature: Idea, Institution, Conflict," in *Author(ity) and the Canon between Institutionalization and Questioning: Literature from High to Late Modernity*, ed. Mihaela Irimia and Dragoș Ivana (Bucharest: Institutul Cultural Român, 2011), 234–43.

11. Hu Shi, "Wenxue jinhua guannian yu xiqu gailiang" 文學進化觀念與戲劇改良 [The concept of literary evolution and theater reform], *Xin qingnian* 新青年 5, no. 4 (October 15, 1918): 311–12. I thank Liu Dong 劉東 for calling this passage to my attention. Hu's contention that contact with foreign literatures is necessary for progress may borrow from Goethe's prediction: "Left to itself every literature will exhaust its vitality, if it is not refreshed by the interest and contributions of a foreign one" (*Goethe's Literary Essays*, ed. Joel Elias Spingarn [New York: Harcourt, Brace, 1921], 92).

12. For an anthology of arguments on the two-way distinction between "Eastern" and "Western" cultures around the time Hu Shi wrote, see Chen Song 陳崧, ed., *Wu si qianhou dongxi wenhua wenti lunzhan wenxuan* 五四前後東西文化問題論戰文選 [An anthology of polemical writings from the May Fourth period referring to the problem of Eastern and Western cultures] (Beijing: Zhongguo shehui kexue chubanshe, 1985). For a discussion of the aporias of this sort of comparison, see Eric Hayot, "Vanishing Horizons: Problems in the Comparison of China and the West," in *A Companion to Comparative Literature*, ed. Ali Behdad and Dominic Thomas (London: Routledge, 2011), 88–107.

13. The whole range of comparison and influence studies obviously exceeds the bounds of the present book. In individual scholars' work, not just familiarity with one or another canon but also a certain model of what constitutes *successful* intercultural communication is apt to dictate the choice of examples. For a fuller picture, see Fang Hao 方豪, *Zhongguo wenxue jiaotongshi luncong: diyiji* 中外文化交通史論叢,

第一輯 [Essays on the history of Chinese-foreign cultural relations, first collection] (Chongqing: Duli chubanshe, 1944); Zhou Faxiang 周發祥 and Li Xiu 李岫, eds., *Zhongwai wenxue jiaoliu shi* 中外文學交流史 [A history of Chinese-foreign literary exchanges] (Changsha: Hunan jiaoyu chubanshe, 1999).

14. In an honorable exception to this rule, a recent number of the *Journal of Chinese Literature and Culture* (7, no. 1, April 2020), edited by Wai-yee Li, was dedicated to the topic of "Cultural Others in Traditional Chinese Literature."

The huge series of international influence studies that burst from the presses of Jinan in 2015, *Zhongwai wenxue jiaoliu shi* 中外文學交流史, with Qian Linsen 錢林森 and Zhou Ning 周寧 as chief editors, ranges farther geographically, potentially enlisting any country on the face of the earth in its single framework. The series so far, published by Jinan's Shandong jiaoyu chubanshe in 2015, comprises Liu Shunli 劉順利, *Zhongwai wenxue jiaoliu shi: Zhongguo-Chaohan juan* 中外文學交流史. 中國—朝韓卷 [History of Chinese-foreign literary exchanges: China-Korea]; Zhou Ning 周寧, *Zhongwai wenxue jiaoliu shi: Zhongguo-Faguo juan* 中外文學交流史. 中國—法國卷 [History of Chinese-foreign literary exchanges: China-France]; Zhao Zhenjiang 趙振江 and Teng Wei 滕威, *Zhongwai wenxue jiaoliu shi: Zhongguo-Xibanyayu guojia juan* 中外文學交流史. 中國—西班牙語國家卷 [History of Chinese-foreign literary exchanges: China and the Spanish-speaking countries]; Zhi Puhao 郅溥浩, Ding Shuhong 丁淑紅, and Zong Xiaofei 宗笑飛, *Zhongwai wenxue jiaoliu shi. Zhongguo-Alabo juan* 中外文學交流史. 中國—阿拉伯卷 [History of Chinese-foreign literary exchanges: China-Arabia]; Liang Lifang 梁麗芳, Ma Jia 馬佳, Zhang Yuhe 张裕禾, and Pu Yazhu 蒲雅竹, *Zhongwai wenxue jiaoliu shi: Zhongguo-Jianada juan* 中外文學交流史. 中國—加拿大卷 [History of Chinese-foreign literary exchanges: China-Canada]; Yu Longyu 郁龍余 and Liu Chaohua 劉朝華, *Zhongwai wenxue jiaoliu shi: Zhongguo-Yindu juan* 中外文學交流史. 中國—印度卷 [History of Chinese-foreign literary exchanges: China-India]; Wei Maoping 衛茂平, Chen Hongyan 陳虹嫣, et al., *Zhongwai wenxue jiaoliu shi: Zhongguo-Deguo juan* 中外文學交流史. 中國—德國卷 [History of Chinese-foreign literary exchanges: China-Germany]; Zhang Xiping 張西平 and Ma Xini 馬西尼, assisted by Zhu Jing 朱菁, *Zhongwai wenxue jiaoliu shi: Zhongguo-Yidali juan* 中外文學交流史. 中國—意大利卷 [History of Chinese-foreign literary exchanges: China-Italy]; Wang Xiaoping 王曉平, *Zhongwai wenxue jiaoliu shi: Zhongguo-Riben juan* 中外文學交流史. 中國—日本卷 [History of Chinese-foreign literary exchanges: China-Japan]; Zhou Ning 周寧, Zhu Hui 朱徽, He Changsheng 賀昌盛, and Zhou Yunlong 周雲龍, *Zhongwai wenxue jiaoliu shi: Zhongguo-Meiguo juan* 中外文學交流史. 中國—美國卷 [History of Chinese-foreign literary exchanges: China–United States]; Yao Feng 姚風, *Zhongwai wenxue jiaoliu shi: Zhongguo-Putaoya juan* 中外文學交流史. 中國—葡萄牙卷 [History of Chinese-foreign literary exchanges: China-Portugal]; Guo Huifen 郭惠芬, *Zhongwai wenxue jiaoliu shi: Zhongguo-Dongnan Ya juan* 中外文學交流史. 中國—東南亞卷 [History of Chinese-foreign literary exchanges: China–Southeast Asia]; Ge Guilu 葛桂錄, *Zhongwai wenxue jiaoliu shi: Zhongguo-Yingguo juan* 中外文學交流史. 中國——英國卷 [History of Chinese-foreign literary exchanges: China-England]. Though credibly multinational and prima facie valuable as documentation, this history is imagined in a formulaic, positivist way: it sees "literary exchange" as occurring on a country-to-country basis and registers it in proofs of translation or imitation, leaving unasked the question of what a country is, whether countries have always existed or exist in some necessary way for literature, and whether influence is so easily documented.

15. On attempts to capture those contextual, specialized, and allusive meanings, see John J. Deeney, "Foundations for Critical Understanding: The Compilation and Translation of Encyclopedic Dictionaries of Chinese Literary Terminology," in *Translating Chinese Literature*, ed. Eugene Eoyang and Lin Yao-fu (Bloomington: Indiana University Press, 1995), 315–42. For a skeptical view, see C. H. Wang, "Naming and Reality of Chinese Criticism," *Journal of Asian Studies* 3 (1979): 529–34. For an argument integrating these moves into a larger historical pattern, see Hayot, "Vanishing Horizons," 97–102.

16. See Daniel J. Simons and Christopher F. Chabris, "Gorillas in Our Midst: Sustained Inattentional Blindness for Dynamic Events," *Perception* 28 (1999): 1059–74. On the various ways of attending to "Asia" and the relevant national "Others" for members of contemporary Asian cultures, see Lo Kwai-Cheung, "When China Encounters Asia Again: Rethinking Ethnic Excess in Some Recent Films from the PRC," *China Review* 10, no. 2 (2010): 63–88, esp. 71–76; and Kuan-Hsing Chen, *Asia as Method: Toward Deimperialization* (Durham, NC: Duke University Press, 2010), 211–55.

17. Hayot, "Vanishing Horizons," 104.

18. I have found encouragement for this task in Édouard Glissant, *Poétique de la relation* (Paris: Gallimard, 1990), translated by Betsy Wing as *Poetics of Relation* (Ann Arbor: University of Michigan Press, 1997); and Bruno Latour, *Enquête sur les modes d'existence: Une anthropologie des Modernes* (Paris: La Découverte, 2012), translated by Catherine Porter as *An Inquiry into Modes of Existence* (Cambridge, MA: Harvard University Press, 2013).

19. See Christopher Bush, "The Other of the Other? Cultural Studies, Theory, and the Location of the Modernist Signifier," *Comparative Literature Studies* 42 (2005): 162–80. Bush offers "a way of reading the formal experiments of literary modernism as a legible site of negotiation between the internal otherness later identified with Theory and the other otherness of cultural difference" (164). The heuristic applies to more than literary modernism.

Chapter 1: The Nine Relays

1. On this subject, see, e.g., Wang Zuoliang 王佐良, *Zhongwai wenxue zhi jian* 中外文學之間 [Between Chinese and foreign literatures] (Nanjing: Jiangsu renmin chubanshe, 1984); Ge Baoquan 戈寶權, *Zhongwai wenxue yinyuan: Ge Baoquan bijiao*

wenxue luncong ji 中外文學因緣: 戈寶權比較文學論文集 [Essays on the karmic affinities of Chinese and foreign literatures] (Beijing: Beijing chubanshe, 1992); Leo Takhung Chan, ed., *Twentieth-Century Chinese Translation Theory: Modes, Issues and Debates* (Amsterdam: Benjamins, 2004); Song Binghui 宋炳輝, *Fangfa yu shijian: Zhongwai wenxue guanxi yanjiu* 方法與實踐: 中外文學關係研究 [Methods and practices: A study of Chinese and foreign literary relations] (Shanghai: Fudan daxue chubanshe, 2004); Eva Hung and Judy Wakabayashi, eds., *Asian Translation Traditions* (2005; reprinted, London: Routledge, 2014); Luo Xuanmin and He Yuanjian, eds., *Translating China* (Boston: Multilingual Matters, 2009); Mark Gamsa, *The Reading of Russian Literature in China: A Moral Example and Manual of Practice* (New York: Palgrave, 2010); Michael Gibbs Hill, *Lin Shu, Inc.: Translation and the Making of Modern Chinese Culture* (Oxford: Oxford University Press, 2012); Lawrence Wangchi Wong, ed., *Translation and Modernization in East Asia in the Nineteenth and Early Twentieth Centuries* (Hong Kong: Research Centre for Translation, 2017); Luo Xuanmin 羅選民, *Fanyi yu Zhongguo xiandaixing* 翻譯與中國現代性 [Translation and Chinese modernity] (Beijing: Qinghua daxue chubanshe, 2017).

2. Liang Qichao, "Fanyi wenxue yu fodian" [Translation literature and the Buddhist classics, 1920], in Liang, *Yinbingshi wenji* 飲冰室文集 (Shanghai: Zhonghua shuju, 1926), 61/1a–24b.

3. Xie Shaobo, "Translating Modernity towards Translating China," in Luo and He, *Translating China*, 135–56; Lydia H. Liu, *Translingual Practice: Literature, National Culture, and Translated Modernity* (Stanford, CA: Stanford University Press, 1992).

4. Lawrence Venuti, *The Translator's Invisibility: A History of Translation*, 2nd ed. (New York: Routledge, 1995, 2008). The remark about Pound being "the inventor of Chinese poetry for our time" is by Eliot; see Timothy Billings, *Cathay: A Critical Edition* (New York: Fordham University Press, 2019), 15.

5. A contemporary example of such pragmatic bilingualism is foregrounded in the film *Lubian yecan* 路邊野餐 (2015; translated as *Kaili Blues*), directed by Bi Gan 畢贛, in which the protagonist, a resident of Guizhou, voices in dialect the poems he writes in standard Chinese. I thank Wang Yaqi 王雅琪 for this reference.

6. Robert Phillipson, "The Linguistic Imperialism of Neoliberal Empire," *Critical Inquiry in Language Studies* 5 (2008): 1–43. See also Aamir R. Mufti, *Forget English! Orientalisms and World Literatures* (Cambridge, MA: Harvard University Press, 2016). On the spread of languages and media, see Alexander Beecroft, *An Ecology of World Literature: From Antiquity to the Present Day* (London: Verso, 2015). On the necessity of remembering China's imperial history and the position it creates for marginal or hybrid populations, see Shu-mei Shih, "The Concept of the Sinophone," *PMLA* 126 (2011): 709–18.

7. See Peter Kornicki, *Language, Scripts, and Chinese Texts in East Asia* (Oxford: Oxford University Press, 2018); Zev Handel, *Sinography: The Borrowing and Adaptation of the Chinese Script* (Leiden: Brill, 2019).

8. See Indra Levy, ed., *Translation in Modern Japan* (New York: Routledge, 2011); Gamsa, *The Reading of Russian Literature in China.*

9. See Paul Grice, "Logic and Conversation," in Grice, *Studies in the Way of Words* (Cambridge, MA: Harvard University Press, 1991), 22–40; Jürgen Habermas, *The Theory of Communicative Action*, trans. Thomas McCarthy, 2 vols. (Boston: Beacon, 1981, 1984).

10. *Mao shi* 205, "Bei shan" 北山.

11. *Mencius*, 1 A 6.

12. Haun Saussy, *Translation as Citation: Zhuangzi Inside Out* (Oxford: Oxford University Press, 2018), 84–88. For another account, see Chun-chieh Huang, *The Debate and Confluence between Confucianism and Buddhism in East Asia*, trans. Jan Vrhovski (Göttingen: V&R unipress, 2020), 37–42. The phrase "ninefold translation" had a long past by Huan Xuan's time: see *Shiji* 123 ("Dayuan zhuan"), and Han Ying 韓嬰, *Hanshi waizhuan* 韓詩外傳 (Shanghai: Shangwu, 1922), 5.13. In both passages, the phrase arises in the context of the Chinese sovereign's prestige being recognized from afar.

13. On Ricci's *shanren* avatar, see Matteo Ricci, *On Friendship: One Hundred Maxims for a Chinese Prince*, ed. and trans. Timothy Billings (New York: Columbia University Press, 2009), 15–17.

14. See James Scott, *Weapons of the Weak: Everyday Forms of Peasant Resistance* (New Haven, CT: Yale University Press, 1985).

15. Luo Xinzhang, *Fanyi lunji* 翻譯論集 [A collection of writings on translation], 2nd ed. (Beijing: Shangwu, 2015), 3.

16. See Erik Zürcher, *The Buddhist Conquest of China* (Leiden: Brill, 2007), 202–3; Zhou Bokan 周伯戡, "Kuche suochu *Dazhi dulun* xieben canjuan zhi yanjiu—jianlun Jiumoluoshen zhi fanyi" 庫車所出《大智度論》寫本殘卷之研究——兼論鳩摩羅什之 翻譯 [On the Fragmentary Treatise on the Great Perfection of Wisdom from Kucha and on Kumarajiva's translations], *Guoli Taiwan daxue lishixue xi xuebao* 17 (1992): 65–106.

17. Dao'an, "*Mohe boluoruo boluomi jing* chao xu," 摩訶鉢羅若波羅蜜經抄序, cited in Sengyou 僧祐, *Chu sanzang jiji xu* 出三藏記集序 8 (T 2145), in *Taishō shinshū Daizōkyō* 大正新脩大藏經, ed. Takakusu Junjirō 高楠順次郎 et al., 100 vols. (Tokyo: Taishō Issaikyō kankōkai, 1924–1932), 55:52b–c.

18. Dao'an, "From the Preface to *A Collation of the Perfection of Great Wisdom Sutra*," trans. Haun Saussy, in *The Translation Studies Reader*, ed. Lawrence Venuti, 4th ed. (New York: Routledge, 2021), 27–28. For alternative translations, see Martha P. Y. Cheung, ed., *An Anthology of Chinese Discourse on Translation*, 2 vols., 2nd ed. (London: Routledge, 2014), 1:79–83; and Christoph Harbsmeier, "Early Chinese Buddhist Translators on Translation: A Brief Introduction with Textual Data," in *La Traduction dans l'histoire des idées linguistiques: représentations et pratiques*, ed. Émilie Aussant (Paris: Geuthner, 2015), 262–64. The prolixity and lack of internal organization that Chinese

readers saw in foreign texts is brought forth as a problem several times in one of the first explicit comparisons of the virtues of Buddhism, Daoism, and Confucianism, the *Mouzi Lihuolun* 牟子理惑論 [Mouzi's discourses for relieving doubts, ca. 200 CE]: see Béatrice Haridon, trans., *Meou-tseu: Dialogues pour dissiper la confusion* (Paris: Les Belles Lettres, 2017), 14–17, 39–40, 47–51.

19. Robert Clouse, dir., *Enter the Dragon* (DVD; Burbank, CA: Warner Brothers Home Video, 1998). The phrase in the original is "fighting without fighting."

20. For a version of the maximal claim about translation, see George Steiner, *After Babel: Aspects of Language and Translation* (Oxford: Oxford University Press, 1975), 47, 198.

21. Handel, *Sinography*, 81–82, citing John Whitman, "The Ubiquity of the Gloss," *Scripta* 3 (2011): 95–121. On glossing and script genesis, see David B. Lurie, *Realms of Literacy: Early Japan and the History of Writing* (Cambridge, MA: Harvard University Asia Center, 2011), esp. 169–212; Kin Bunkyō, *Literary Sinitic and East Asia: A Culture Sphere of Vernacular Reading*, trans. Ross King, Marjorie Burge, Si Nae Park, Alexy Luschenko, and Mina Hattori (Leiden: Brill, 2021). For a detailed study of oral and aural vernacularization of Chinese texts, see Si Nae Park, "The Sound of Learning the Confucian *Classics* in Chosŏn Korea," *Harvard Journal of Asiatic Studies* 79 (2019): 131–87. On the career of certain Chinese literary works in Korea and Japan, see Zhang Bowei 張伯偉, *Dong Ya Hanji yanjiu lunji* 東亞漢籍研究論集 [Essays on Han-character writings in East Asia] (Taipei: Taida chubanzhongxin, 2007); and *Yuwai Hanji yanjiu rumen* 域外漢籍研究入門 [An introduction to Han-character writings outside China] (Shanghai: Fudan daxue chubanshe, 2012); as well as Bian Dongbo 卞東波, *Yuwai Hanji yu Songdai wenxue yanjiu* 域外漢籍與宋代文學研究 [Han-character writings outside China and Song-dynasty literature] (Beijing: Zhonghua shuju, 2017). On the several different types of glossing or vernacularization in use, and on the eventual identification by Meiji reformers of Chinese characters as a foreign body in Japanese writing, see Atsuko Ueda, "Sound, Scripts, and Styles: *Kanbun Kundokutai* and the National Language Reforms of 1880s Japan," *Review of Japanese Culture and Society* 20 (2008): 133–56. On the extension of *kundoku* glossing practices in Japan to languages other than Chinese, see Matthew Fraleigh, "Rearranging the Figures on the Tapestry: What Japanese Direct Translation of European Texts Can Tell Us about *kanbun kundoku*," *Japan Forum* 31 (2019): 4–32.

22. See, for example, "Gaogouli" 高句麗, chap. 100 in Wei Shou 魏收, comp., *Wei shu* 魏書 (Beijing: Zhonghua shuju, 1974), 6:2213–17; "Dong yi: Gaoli" 東夷高麗, chap. 81 in Wei Zheng 魏徵, comp., *Sui shu* 隋書 [History of the Sui dynasty] (Beijing: Zhonghua shuju, 1973), 6:1813–17.

23. On Qian's interest in Korea, see Sixiang Wang, "Loyalty, History, and Empire: Qian Qianyi and His Korean Biographies," in *Representing Lives in China: Forms of Biography in the Ming-Qing Period 1368–1911*, ed. Ihor Pidhainy, Roger Des Forges, and Grace S. Fong (Ithaca, NY: Cornell University East Asia Series, 2019), 299–32.

24. The Manchu invasion in 1644 and subsequent occupation of China led Korean and Japanese observers to conclude that "since the end of the Ming, there has been no China" 明朝後無中國. See Ge Zhaoguang 葛兆光, *He wei Zhongguo? Jiangyu, minzu, wenhua yu lishi* 何為中國？疆域、民族、文化與歷史 (Hong Kong: Oxford University Press, 2014), 149; Ge Zhaoguang, *What Is China? Territory, Ethnicity, Culture and History,* trans. Michael Gibbs Hill (Cambridge, MA: Harvard University Press, 2018), 125. The shocking collapse of the Ming and the condition of "Hua and Yi exchanging positions" (*Hua Yi biantai / Ka I hentai* 華夷變態), in Hayashi Gahō's 林鵞峰 (1618–1680) formulation, meant that the cultural legitimacy denoted by "Zhongguo" or "Tianxia" was no longer bound to its places of origin and could be applied to any domain where civilization, as Confucians conceived of it, was preserved. On the crisis of naming and protocol that the fall of the Ming represented for Korean cultural-political fealty, see Sun Weiguo 孫衛國, *Da Ming qihao yu xiao Zhonghua yishi: Chaoxian wangchao zun Zhou si Ming wenti yanjiu, 1637–1800* 大明旗號與小中華意識：朝鮮王朝尊周思明問題研究, 1637–1800 [The national designation of the Great Ming and the consciousness of being "little China": Studies on the Chosŏn dynasty's reverence for the Zhou and nostalgia for the Ming, 1637–1800] (Beijing: Shangwu, 2007); and Yuanchong Wang, "Civilizing the Great Qing: Manchu-Korean Relations and the Reconstruction of the Chinese Empire, 1644–1761," *Late Imperial China* 38 (2017): 113–54. For a consideration in the broad perspective of Chinese history, see Arif Dirlik, "Born in Translation: 'China' in the Making of 'Zhongguo,'" *boundary 2* 46 (2019): 121–52. On the claims to legitimacy of the short-lived successor state of Southern Ming under Koxinga (Zheng Chenggong 鄭成功, 1624–1662), see Yang Rubin (Yang Rur-bin 楊儒賓), "Ming Zheng wanghou wu Zhongguo" 明鄭亡後無中國 [On the "loss of China" after the end of the Ming Koxinga resistance], *Zhongzheng hanxue yanjiu* 31 (2018): 1–32, esp. 26–27.

25. Conventional English translations for these terms are "benevolence," "loyalty," "the Doctrine of the Mean," "the Mandate of Heaven," and the "Three Obediences and Four Virtues" required of women.

26. The sense of "inscription" with which I work was articulated by Paul de Man. See Tom Cohen, Barbara Cohen, J. Hillis Miller, and Andrzej Warminski, eds., *Material Events: Paul de Man and the Afterlife of Theory* (Minneapolis: University of Minnesota Press, 2001).

27. Charles Holcombe, *The Genesis of East Asia, 221 B.C.–A.D. 907* (Honolulu: University of Hawai'i Press, 2001), 66.

28. Wei Zheng, comp., *Sui shu*, chap. 81, 6:1815.

29. Both groups had declared fealty to the Sui; it appears that Goguryeo had been interfering in their contacts with the Sui court.

30. Alluding to *Mencius* 3 A 5.

31. Wei Zheng, *Sui shu*, chap. 81, 6:1815. Tang (r. 559–590) is known in Korean historiography by his formal name, Pyeongwon-wang 平原王.

32. See Mark Byington, "The War of Words between South Korea and China over an Ancient Kingdom," *History News Network*, September 10, 2004, http://historynewsnetwork.org/article/7077#sthash.rsCQE73r.dpuf.

33. Wei Zheng, *Sui shu*, 6:1814–15.

34. Kornicki, *Language, Scripts, and Chinese Texts*; Handel, *Sinography*; Kin, *Literary Sinitic and East Asia*.

35. *Kaifūsō* 懷風藻 63, as translated in H. Mack Horton, *Traversing the Frontier: The Man'yōshū Account of a Japanese Mission to Silla in 736–737* (Cambridge, MA: Harvard University Asia Center, 2012), 308–9. (This poem by a Japanese dignitary celebrates a mission from Silla a few years before the embassy recorded in the *Man'yōshū*.) Underlined expressions refer to *Shijing* poems 163 and 161.

36. Nakanishi Susumu 中西進, ed., *Man'yōshū* 萬葉集 (Tokyo: Kodansha, 1978), 15.3676. I thank Zhang Yan 張豔 for locating the triple text. On the *Man'yōshū*'s place in the history of Japanese writing, between logography and phonography, see Lurie, *Realms of Literacy*, 271–308.

37. *Man'yōshū* 15.3676, as translated in Horton, *Traversing the Frontier*, 33. The goose refers to the Han-dynasty general Su Wu's captivity among the Xiongnu: he tied a note to the foot of a migrating goose and so let the people in the Han capital know he was still alive.

38. John Timothy Wixted, "The *Kokinshū* Prefaces: Another Perspective," *Harvard Journal of Asiatic Studies* 43 (1983): 238. See also Wiebke Denecke, *Classical World Literatures: Sino-Japanese and Greco-Roman Comparisons* (New York: Oxford University Press, 2014), 62–72. For a similar double preface proclaiming the legitimacy of Sinographic and local (Vietnamese) writing alike, see John Phan, "Chữ Nôm and the Taming of the South: A Bilingual Defense for Vernacular Writing in the *Chỉ Nam Ngọc Âm Giải Nghĩa*," *Journal of Vietnamese Studies* 8 (2013): 1–33.

39. The 1592 ethnographic work *Riben fengtu ji* 日本風土記 [The land and customs of Japan] by Hou Jigao 侯繼高 contains the earliest known Chinese discussion of Japanese *waka* poetry. See Yuanfei Wang, *Writing Pirates: Vernacular Fiction and Oceans in Late Ming China* (Ann Arbor: University of Michigan Press, 2021), 104–8.

Chapter 2: Can the Barbarians Sing?

1. See, for example, Ge Zhaoguang, *He wei Zhongguo?* and *What Is China?*; Sanping Chen, *Multicultural China in the Early Middle Ages* (Philadelphia: University of Pennsylvania Press, 2012); Jonathan Karam Skaff, *Sui-Tang China and Its Turco-Mongol Neighbors: Culture, Power, and Connections, 580–800* (Oxford: Oxford University Press, 2012); Shao-yun Yang, *The Way of the Barbarians: Redrawing Ethnic Boundaries in Tang and Song China* (Seattle: University of Washington Press, 2019). For a comparative literary perspective, see Cao Shunqing, "Research on the Literature

of National Minorities under Three Discourse Hegemonies," *Comparative Literature: East & West* 1, no. 2 (2017): 145–56.

2. More precisely: "Music brings together what is (or should be) similar; ritual distinguishes what is (or should be) different" 樂合同，禮別異. Xunzi, "Yue lun" 樂論 [A discourse on music], in *Xunzi jijie* 荀子集解, ed. Wang Xianqian 王先謙, *Xinbian zhuzi jicheng* 新編諸子集成 (1936; reprint, Taipei, 1986), 2:255.

3. *Zhou li* [*Rites of Zhou*], *Sibucongkan chubian* 四部叢刊初編 edition, juan 3, 5a.

4. See Yu Siu-wah 余少華 (Yu Shaohua), "Zhongguo yinyue de bianyuan: shaoshuminzu yinyue" 中國音樂的邊緣：少數民族音樂 [The margins of Chinese music: Minority music], in *Biancheng duihua: Xianggang, Zhongguo, bianyuan, bianjie* 邊城對話: 香港．中國．邊緣．邊界 (*City on the Frontier: Hong Kong, China, Boundaries and Borderland*), ed. Pang Laikwan 彭麗君 (Peng Lijun) (Hong Kong: Chinese University Press, 2013), 59–95. I am indebted to Yu for much of the discussion of this passage. For *didi*, see *Li ji*, "Wang zhi" 王制 [The royal institutions], in *Shisan jing zhushu*, 5:2894. On the semantic field of titles attributed to translators, see Wolfgang Behr, "'To Translate' Is 'to Exchange' 譯者言易也: Linguistic Diversity and the Terms for Translation in Ancient China," in *Mapping Meanings: The Field of New Learning in Late Qing China*, ed. Michael Lackner and Natascha Vittinghoff (Leiden: Brill, 2004), 199–235, esp. 212–23.

5. Chen Li 陳立, ed., *Baihu tong shuzheng* 白虎通疏證 (Beijing: Zhonghua shuju, 1994), 1:107–8.

6. Chen Li, *Baihu tong shuzheng*, 1:108–9.

7. Chen Li, *Baihu tong shuzheng*, 1:110–11.

8. *Zhouli shu* 周禮疏 [The Rites of Zhou, annotated], cited in Chen Li, ed., *Baihu tong shuzheng*, 111.

9. Han Yu, "Yuan dao" 原道 [Tracing the origins of the way], in *Han Changli wenji jiaozhu* 韓昌黎文集校注 [Selected prose of Han Yu], ed. Ma Tongbo 馬通伯 (Hong Kong: Zhonghua shuju, 1991), 7–11.

10. *Zhongyong* 28, as translated by Legge, *The Doctrine of the Mean*, 1:424, with changes. The ideal of script unity was already expressed in the mostly fourth-century BCE *Guanzi* 管子, SBBY edition, ed. Fang Xuanling (Shanghai: Zhonghua shuju, 1930), juan 10, 16a. On its use as a symbol of order in early imperial propaganda, see Martin Kern, *The Stele Inscriptions of Ch'in Shih-huang: Text and Ritual in Early Chinese Imperial Representation* (New Haven, CT: American Oriental Society, 2000), 27–28.

11. *Xunzi jijie*, 2:289–90; translation from Xunzi, "Human Nature Is Bad," in *Xunzi: The Complete Text*, trans. Eric L. Hutton (Princeton, NJ: Princeton University Press, 2014), 248, with slight changes.

12. Lydia H. Liu, *The Clash of Empires: The Invention of China in Modern World-Making* (Cambridge, MA: Harvard University Press, 2004), 3–15. See also Dilip K. Basu, "Chinese Xenology and the Opium War: Reflections on Sinocentrism," *Journal of Asian Studies* 73 (2014): 927–40.

13. Kornicki, *Languages, Scripts, and Chinese Texts*, 6.

14. Matthew W. Mosca, "Neither Chinese nor Outsiders: *Yi* and Non-*Yi* in the Qing Imperial Worldview," *Asia Major*, 3rd series, 33 (2020): 103–46. On the special case of the Yongzheng emperor's edict in response to the scholar Zeng Jing 曾靜 (1679–1736), see 122–38.

15. Elvin Meng alerts me to a bilingual Manchu-Chinese conversation manual of 1809, titled *Manju gisun i oyonggo jorin* 清文指要 (Basics of the Manchu language), in which a Manchu speaker praises his Chinese friend for speaking without a Chinese accent ("majige nikan mudan akv" 一點蠻音沒有)—the unusual thing being the translation of Manchu *nikan*, which normally means "Chinese," by *man* 蠻, sometimes used to designate "foreigners" generally but in classical texts referring specifically to the barbarians of the far South. See Wei Qiaoyan 魏巧燕, "*Qingwen zhiyao*" *zhengli yanjiu*《清文指要》整理研究 [An edition and study of the Basics of the Manchu Language] (Beijing: Peking University Press, 2017), 116.

16. *Mencius* 4 B 1.

17. Jiang Tong, "Xi Rong lun" 徙戎論 [On expelling the barbarians], cited in Fang Xuanling 房玄齡, comp., *Jin shu* 晉書 56, in *Ershiwu shi* 二十五史, 12 vols. (Shanghai: Guji, 1986), 2:1421–22. Jiang paraphrases a passage from *Zuo zhuan*, Duke Zhao, twenty-third year: "In ancient times, the Son of Heaven defended against the Four Yi; when the Son of Heaven became debased, he defended against the various nobles" (*Shisan jing zhushu*, 6:4565).

18. Nicola Di Cosmo, *Ancient China and Its Enemies: The Rise of Nomadic Power in Chinese History* (Cambridge: Cambridge University Press, 2002); Chin, *Savage Exchange*.

19. Erica Fox Brindley, *Ancient China and the Yue: Perceptions and Identities on the Southern Frontier, c. 400 BCE–50 CE* (Cambridge: Cambridge University Press, 2015), 117.

20. Cf. Gayatri Chakravorty Spivak's famous essay, "Can the Subaltern Speak? Speculations on Widow Sacrifice," *Wedge* 7/8 (1985): 120–30.

21. My transliteration into current Mandarin of an ancient Chinese transliteration of the Yue song is merely a convenience here (the Eastern Han pronunciation of the characters being, first of all, a doubtful but unavoidable starting point for reconstructing the Yue sounds). For a careful transcription and study with proposed cognates from Tai-Burmese languages, see Zhengzhang Shangfang 鄭張尚芳, "Decipherment of Yue-Ren-Ge (Song of the Yue Boatman)," *Cahiers de linguistique Asie orientale* 20 (1991): 159–68. For a recent interpretation in the context of regional language and script traditions, see Yen Shih-hsuan 顏世鉉, "A Tentative Discussion of Some Phenomena Concerning Early Texts of the *Shi jing*," *Bamboo and Silk* 4, no. 1 (2021): 59–62.

22. Liu Xiang 劉向, *Shuo yuan* 11.13; also cited in *Yutai xinyong* 玉台新詠9. In *Shuo yuan*, the story about Zixi and the boatman is included as an exemplum in a story about Zhuang Xin and Xiangcheng jun, both nobles of Chu.

23. "What evening is this?," echoes *Mao shi* no. 118, "Chou mou" 綢繆; the motif of shy longing is common to many poems of the *Chu ci* 楚辭 [Songs of the South].

24. "Nanman xinanyi liezhuan" 南蠻西南夷列傳, chap. 86 in *Hou Han shu* 後漢書 [The history of the Later Han dynasty], ed. Fan Ye 范曄, annot. Li Xian 李賢, 12 vols. (Beijing: Zhonghua, 1965), 12:2854–56.

25. W. South Coblin, "A New Study of the Pai-Lang Songs," *Tsinghua Journal of Chinese Studies*, n.s. 12 (1979): 179–215. See also Nathan Wayne Hill, "Songs of the Bailang: A New Transcription with Etymological Commentary," *Bulletin de l'École française d'Extrême-Orient* 103 (2017): 386–429. The exact place of Bailang among the dialects of the trans-Himalayan region is disputed.

26. As Rey Chow has observed, "Imperialism as ideological domination succeeds best without physical coercion, without actually capturing the body and the land": *Writing Diaspora: Tactical Interventions in Contemporary Cultural Studies* (Bloomington: Indiana University Press, 1993), 8. Hence the popularity of "civilizing mission" ideologies among conquering peoples: see Andrew Phillips, "Civilising Missions and the Rise of International Hierarchies in Early Modern Asia," *Millennium—Journal of International Studies* 42 (2014): 697–717, and Edward Vickers, "A Civilising Mission with Chinese Characteristics? Education, Colonialism and Chinese State Formation in Comparative Perspective," in *Constructing Modern Asian Citizenship*, ed. Edward Vickers and Krishna Kumar (London: Routledge, 2015), 50–79.

Whether the apparent formal equivalence between Bailang and Chinese wording in the texts as transcribed is an argument for or against the songs' authenticity I find hard to decide. We have no particular reason to assume that previous Bailang song composition fell into regular four-word lines and fourteen-line stanzas. As with the "Yueren ge," the translator may have adapted to conventions in vogue on the receivers' end. Note also that the *Hou Han shu* gives the Chinese text as principal and the Bailang transcription as commentary, but the *Dongguan ji* inverts this order.

27. *Analects* 6.18.

28. Chen, *Multicultural China in the Early Middle Ages*; Skaff, *Sui-Tang China and Its Turco-Mongol Neighbors*; Wang Zhenping, *Tang China in Multi-Polar Asia: A History of Diplomacy and War* (Honolulu: University of Hawai'i Press, 2013).

29. Li Shimin 李世民 (r. 626–649), cited in Sima Guang 司馬光, chief ed., *Zizhi tongjian* 資治通鑑 (Beijing: Zhonghua, 1956), chap. 197, 3:6215–16. For the reference, I am indebted to Chen Sanping, "A-gan Revisited—The Tuoba's Cultural and Political Heritage," *Journal of Asian History* 30 (1996): 46–78.

30. For a meticulous examination of the use of the categories of ethnicity and orthodoxy in elite internecine struggles, with concentration on the *guwen* 古文 (archaist) movement in the Tang, see Yang, *The Way of the Barbarians*.

31. Guo Maoqian 郭茂倩, *Yuefu shiji* 樂府詩集 (Beijing: Zhonghua, 1979), 86.1212–13. For the origin story, see Li Yanshou 李延壽, comp., *Bei shi* 北史, chap. 6, in *Ershiwu shi*, 4:2917; for Hulü Jin's biography, see Li Baiyao 李百藥, comp., *Bei Qi shu* 北齊書,

chap. 17, in *Ershiwu shi*, 3:2532. Many modern interpreters question the transmitted history of the song. On the history and reception, see David R. Knechtges and Tai-ping Chang, *Ancient and Early Medieval Chinese Literature: A Reference Guide* (Leiden: Brill, 2010), 1:122–24.

32. Luo Yuming, *A Concise History of Chinese Literature*, trans. Yang Ye (Leiden: Brill, 2011), 1:259. For an indication of the stereotypical character of this appreciation, see the travel narrative of Chen Chengzhi 陳澄之, *Yili yanyun lu* 伊犁烟雲錄 [Fugitive impressions of the Yili region] (n.p.: Zhonghua jianguo chubanshe, 1948), 22: "My readers certainly must know the 'Chi-le song' with its 'heavens like a yurt cover / Thrown over the four directions.' So natural, so vast, so sincere!" On expected properties of northern nomad writing, see Lu Kou, "The Epistolary Self and Psychological Warfare: Tuoba Tao's (408–452, r. 423–452) Letters and His Southern Audience," *Journal of Chinese Literature and Culture* 7, no. 1 (2020): 34–59.

33. *Xiandai hanyu guifan cidian* 現代漢語規範辭典, s.v. 敕勒.

34. Wikipedia entry, https://zh.wikipedia.org/wiki/敕勒#《敕勒歌》, consulted June 18, 2019.

35. James C. Scott, *Seeing Like a State: How Certain Schemes to Improve the Human Condition Have Failed* (New Haven, CT: Yale University Press, 1998).

36. *Jin shu* 97.2537 (in *Ershiwu shi*, 2:1540). On the *Jin shu*'s evaluation of the two brothers, see Randolph B. Ford, *Rome, China, and the Barbarians: Ethnographic Traditions and the Transformation of Empires* (Cambridge: Cambridge University Press, 2020), 151–52. As the *Jin shu* observes, "Agan" 阿干 is not a proper name but the Xianbei designation for elder brother. Intermarriage and code-switching brought a cognate of "Agan," *ge* 哥 ("elder brother"), from this Altaic language into the core vocabulary of spoken Chinese from the sixth century onward: see Mei Tsu-Lin 梅祖麟, "Ge zi laiyuan bu zheng" 「哥」字來源補證, in *In Memory of Mantaro J. Hashimoto*, ed. Anne O. Yue and Mitsuaki Endo (Tokyo: Uchiyama Shoten, 1997), 97–101.

37. Huang Jianzhong 黃建中 and Wu Dingxin 吳鼎新, eds., *Gaolan xianzhi* 皋蘭縣志 (1775), accessed through ctext.org. Thomas D. Carroll, SJ, *Account of the T'ŭ-Yü-Hún in the History of the Chín Dynasty* (Berkeley: University of California Press, 1953), 18, likewise admits that he can find no text for the song earlier than the late Qing.

38. See book 3 of Gaius Julius Caesar, *Commentarii de Bello Gallico*, ed. Heinrich Meusel, 3 vols. (Berlin: Weidmann, 1961). On Greek ethnocentrism generally, see Arnaldo Momigliano, *Alien Wisdom: The Limits of Hellenization* (Cambridge: Cambridge University Press, 1975).

39. Liu Xu 劉昫, comp., *Jiu Tang shu* 舊唐書, chap. 29, "Yin yue zhi" 音樂志, part 2, in *Ershiwu shi*, 5:3614; also found in *Taiping yulan* 太平御覽, 70.1.32, and *Yuefu shiji*, 25.363. For the characteristics of "horseback music," along with a specious derivation from the cosmic conflict of the Yellow Emperor and Chiyou 蚩尤, see *Jin shu*, chap. 23, "Yue zhi" 樂志, in *Ershiwu shi*, 2:1325. "Khan" 可汗 in the quoted passage may be

equivalent to "Agan" in the *Jin shu* song title. Parts of the passage omitted here eluci-
date the means of preserving repertoire in the music agencies of the court over centuries by hereditary clans of musicians, often going back to foreign ancestors. On the
remarkable consistency of representations of "alien" or "minority" music in China
from the *Rituals of Zhou* to the present, see Yu Siu-wah, "Zhongguo yinyue de
bianyuan."

40. Thousands of scrolls in a variety of Central Asian languages were discovered
in the so-called Library Cave of the Mogao Grottoes in Dunhuang around 1900.
Many were acquired by European libraries and museums; digital scanning and sharing is now reassembling the collection. See the International Dunhuang Project
housed at the British Library, http://idp.bl.uk.

41. On such issues, see Haun Saussy, "Review Essay: Recent Chinese Literary
Histories in English," *Harvard Journal of Asiatic Studies* 79 (2019): 231–48; "The Comparative History of East Asian Literatures: A Sort of Manifesto," *Modern Languages
Open* 1 (2018), 20, https://www.modernlanguagesopen.org/articles/10.3828/mlo
.v0i0.206/.

Chapter 3: The *Hanzi wenhua quan*

1. Joseph R. Allen, "The Babel Fallacy: When Translation Does Not Matter," *Cultural Critique* 102 (2019): 117.

2. Luo Xinzhang, *Fanyi lilun*, 1. On Luo's construction of Chinese translation
theory, see Martha P. Y. Cheung, "Power and Ideology in Translation Research in
Twentieth-Century China: An Analysis of Three Seminal Works," in *Crosscultural
Transgressions: Research Models in Translation Studies, II: Historical and Ideological
Issues*, ed. Theo Hermans (Manchester, UK: St. Jerome, 2002), 160.

3. Liang Qichao 梁啟超, "Fanyi wenxue yu fodian" 翻譯文學與佛典 (1920), in
Yinbingshi wenji 飲冰室文集 (Shanghai: Zhonghua shuju, 1926), 3a.

4. See, for the sake of analogy, Talal Asad, Judith Butler, and Saba Mahmood, *Is
Critique Secular? Blasphemy, Injury, and Free Speech* (New York: Fordham University
Press, 2009).

5. Wiebke Denecke, "Worlds without Translation: Premodern East Asia and the
Power of Character Scripts," in *A Companion to Translation Studies*, ed. Sandra Bermann and Catherine Porter (Chichester, UK: Wiley, 2014), 205. For different views
on *kundoku* and translation, see Ueda, "Sound, Scripts, and Styles," and Fraleigh,
"Rearranging the Figures on the Tapestry." On the purported unity of the Chinese-
character civilization, see Lurie, *Realms of Literacy*, 348–53, 417–18.

6. Yukino Semizu, "Invisible Translation: Reading Chinese Texts in Ancient
Japan," in *Translating Others*, ed. Theo Hermans (Manchester, UK: St. Jerome, 2006),
2:283–95.

7. Denecke, "Worlds without Translation," 214. In this case, it would seem that written Chinese became a "phonetic script" in the hands of such writers as Han Bangqing 韓邦慶, for the Suzhou-dialect speech of his novel *Hai shang hua liezhuan* 海上花列傳 (1892) was "annotated/translated" (*zhuyi* 註譯, as the title page states) into Mandarin by Eileen Chang some ninety years later. See Han Bangqing, *Hai shang hua* 海上花, trans. Zhang Ailing 張愛玲 (Taipei: Huangguan zazhi she, 1983).

8. On the internal divisions of the "Sinosphere," see Hu Siao-chen 胡曉真, "Fengsheng yu wenzi: cong geyao yundong huisi fei Hanyu de hanzi chuanshu" 風聲與文字：從歌謠運動回思非漢語的漢字傳述 [Popular airs and the written word: Thinking back from the folksong movement to the Han-character transmission of non-Han texts], *Zhongguo wenzhe yanjiu tongxun* 29 (2019): 53–77. For a discussion of national identity and script, see Chiung Wi-vun (Jiang Weiwen) 蔣為文, "Cong Hanzi wenhua quan kan yuyan wenzi yu guojia rentong zhi guanxi," 從漢字文化圈看語言文字與國家認同之關係 [Viewing language, writing and national identity from the Sinographic culture sphere], conference paper presented in June 2006, http://www.de-han.org/phenglun/2006/bunhoalunsoat.pdf. More broadly, the "Sinophone" approach to literary history has persistently questioned centralizing narratives about Chinese modernity: see, for example, Shih, "The Concept of the Sinophone"; Jing Tsu, *Sound and Script in Chinese Diaspora* (Cambridge, MA: Harvard University Press, 2010); David Der-Wei Wang, "Sinophone Intervention with China: Between National and World Literature," in *Texts and Transformations: Essays in Honor of Victor Mair's 75th Birthday*, ed. Haun Saussy (Amherst, NY: Cambria Press, 2018), 59–79.

9. Kornicki, *Languages, Scripts, and Chinese Texts*; Handel, *Sinography*. See also Sowon S. Park, "Introduction: Transnational Scriptworlds," *Journal of World Literature* 1 (2016): 129–41, and the other essays in that journal special issue.

10. On the many functions of script and their irreducibility to a goal-oriented process, see Lurie, *Realms of Literacy*, esp. 358–64. On the effects of changes in script protocols on the transmission of manuscript editions, see Horton, *Traversing the Frontier*, 191, 196, 407–9.

11. Kornicki, *Languages, Scripts, and Chinese Texts*, 183, citing Imre Galambos, *Translating Chinese Tradition and Teaching Tangut Culture: Manuscripts and Printed Books from Khara-Khoto* (Berlin: de Gruyter, 2015).

12. Galambos, *Translating Chinese Tradition*, 134.

13. *Yuanchao mishi*, *Sibu congkan* edition (Shanghai: Shangwu, 1936), 1/1a.

14. For details on the compilation and versions of the *Secret History*, see Igor de Rachewiltz, trans. and comm., *The Secret History of the Mongols: A Mongolian Epic Chronicle of the Thirteenth Century*, 3 vols. (Leiden: Brill, 2004–2013), 1:xxix, xxxiii, xl–xlviii; and Bai Temuerbagen 白特木爾巴根, "*Menggu mishi*" wenxian banben kao 《蒙古秘史》文獻版本考 (Beijing: Peking University Press, 2014), 22–29, 72–77.

For "mined," see de Rachewiltz, *The Secret History*, xlvi. For an edition of the Mongolian glossary, see Huo Yuanjie 火源潔, trans., *Hua Yi yiyu* (Shanghai: Shangwu, 1926). On the processes of translation, transcription, and performance that surrounded the writing of the history and the glossaries, see Carla Nappi, *Translating Early Modern China: Illegible Cities* (Oxford: Oxford University Press, 2021).

15. Li Wentian 李文田, ed., *Yuanchao mishi*, *Congshu jicheng* edition (Shanghai: Shangwu, 1935). On the Mongol empire's human infrastructures, see Michal Biran, "Mobility, Empire and Cross-Cultural Contacts in Cross-Cultural Eurasia," *Medieval Worlds* 8 (2018): 135–54. And on Ming ways of dealing with the Mongol legacy, see David Robinson, "Mongolian Migration and the Ming's Place in Asia," *Journal of Central Eurasian Studies* 3 (2019): 109–29, and "Controlling Memory and Movement: The Early Ming Court and the Changing Chinggisid World," *Journal of the Economic and Social History of the Orient* 62 (2019): 503–24.

16. *Huainanzi* 16, in *Huainan honglie jijie* 淮南鴻烈集解, ed. Liu Wendian 劉文典, 2 vols. (Beijing: Zhonghua shuju, 1989), 2:542.

17. See Sima Qian, chap. 83 of *Shiji*, 8:2478. Zhaoge was the capital of the state of Wei 衛; the location of Shengmu is unknown. For a fine short discussion of the significance of local languages in Chinese history, see Zhou Zhenhe 周振鶴, "Cong fangyan rentong, minzu yuyan rentong dao gongtongyu rentong" 從方言認同，民族語言認同到共通語認同 [From the identities of dialects and folk languages to the identity of a common language], 192–206, in Zhou Zhenhe, *Yu shi ruo jue* 余事若覺 (Beijing: Zhonghua shuju, 2012).

18. Wang Chong, *Lunheng* 論衡, chap. 16 (Taipei: Shijie shuju, 1983), 68.

19. Lawrence Yim, "Exile, Borders, and Poetry: A Study of Fang Xiaobiao's 'Miscellaneous Poems on the Eastern Journey,'" *Journal of Chinese Literature and Culture* 7, no. 1 (2020): 192–214.

20. *Zhongyong*. Dagmar Schäfer indicates that "by the late twentieth century, state and intellectual actors utilised the seeming incommensurability [with other languages] of Classical Chinese terms in identity building debates," citing Guo Yangsheng, "Theorizing the Politics of Translation in a Global Era: A Chinese Perspective," *Translator* 15, no. 2 (2009): 239–59. The *hanzi wenhua quan* may be another such identity-building device for the East Asia region. See Schäfer, "Translation History, Knowledge and Nation Building in China," in *The Routledge Handbook of Translation and Culture*, ed. Sue-Ann Harding and Ovidi Carbonelli Cortés (London: Routledge, 2018), 135.

21. John Whitman, "The Ubiquity of the Gloss," cited in Kornicki, *Languages, Scripts, and Chinese Texts*, 184.

22. Kornicki, *Languages, Scripts, and Chinese Texts*, 166.

23. Emanuel Pastreich, "Grappling with Chinese Writing as a Material Language: Ogyū Sorai's *Yakubunsentei*," *Harvard Journal of Asiatic Studies* 61 (2001): 119–70. See also Lurie, *Realms of Literacy*, 332–33.

24. Kornicki, *Languages, Scripts, and Chinese Texts*, 179.

25. Ueda, "Sound, Scripts, and Styles," 142.

26. Liam C. Kelley, *Beyond the Bronze Pillars: Envoy Poetry and the Sino-Vietnamese Relationship* (Honolulu: Association for Asian Studies and University of Hawai'i Press, 2005), 13, citing and paraphrasing O. W. Wolters, "Assertions of Cultural Well-being in Fourteenth-Century Vietnam," *Journal of Southeast Asian Studies* 10 (1979): 435–50, and 11 (1980): 74–90. On the divergent perspectives of Alexander Woodside and O. W. Wolters, with historiographical examples tending to confirm Wolters's position, see Shawn McHale, "'Texts and Bodies': Refashioning the Disturbing Past of Tran Vietnam (1225–1400)," *Journal of the Economic and Social History of the Orient* 42 (1999): 494–518.

27. Schäfer, "Translation History, Knowledge and Nation Building in China," 139.

28. Kornicki, *Languages, Scripts, and Chinese Texts*, 213. For examples of Chinese literary exports to Korea and Japan, see Zhang Bowei, *Dong Ya Hanji yanjiu lunji*, and Bian Dongbo, *Yuwai Hanji yu Songdai wenxue yanjiu*.

29. Kornicki, *Languages, Scripts, and Chinese Texts*, 303, 18. For information on medieval Vietnamese exiles and refugees in Korea, see David W. Kim, "A Satirical Legend or Transnational History: The Vietnamese Royal Narrative in Medieval Koryŏ," *ChiMoKoJa: Histories of China, Mongolia, Korea and Japan* 3 (2018): 1–19.

30. On the Southwest, see Hu Siao-chen (Hu Xiaozhen) 胡曉真, *Ming-Qing wenxue zhong de xinan xushi* 明清文學中的西南敘事 [Narratives of the Southwest in Ming and Qing literature] (Taipei: Taida chuban zhongxin, 2019). On Ming debates surrounding policies toward southern tribal peoples, in particular whether and how to "civilize" them, see, for example, Leo K. Shin, "The Last Campaigns of Wang Yang-ming," *T'oung Pao* 2nd series, 92, fasc. 1/3 (2006): 101–28.

31. See David Holm, *Mapping the Old Zhuang Character Script: A Vernacular Writing System from Southern China* (Leiden: Brill, 2013); Jingqi Fu, Zhao Min, Xu Lin, and Duan Ling, *Chinese Ethnic Minority Oral Traditions: A Recovered Text of Bai Folk Songs in a Sinoxenic Script* (Amherst, NY: Cambria Press, 2015); Wilt Idema, *Heroines of Jiangyong: Chinese Narrative Ballads in Women's Script* (Seattle: University of Washington Press, 2009).

32. *Jiu Tang shu* 舊唐書, chap. 196a, in *Ershiwu shi*, 5:4105. For the story of the Prince of Dongping, see Ban Gu 班固, *Han shu* 漢書, chap. 80 (Beijing: Zhonghua shuju, 1962), 6:3324–25. On book circulation generally, see Talbott Huey, "Chinese Books as Cultural Exports from Han to Ming: A Bibliographic Essay," *Studies on Asia*, series 3, vol. 3, no. 1 (2006), https://www.eiu.edu/studiesonasia/series_iii_3.php.

33. "Rong," a term used in antiquity for warlike outsiders from the west, is here made to serve as an ethnonym for the Tibetans.

34. To shift the ground of the discussion slightly, Yu Xiulie is also asserting that Tang policies are in fact based on these ancient classical texts—which may or may not be true but may have been the right thing to say, indeed especially if it were not

self-evidently true. I thank an anonymous reader for the press for suggesting this line of inquiry.

35. For a fuller citation, see chapter 2, note 9.

36. See Su Shi 蘇軾, "Lun Gaoli mai shu lihai zhazi sanshou" 論高麗買書利害劄子三首 [Three memoranda on the advantages and disadvantages of selling books to Korea], in Su Shi wenji 蘇軾文集, ed. Kong Fanli 孔凡禮, 6 vols. (Beijing: Zhonghua, 1986), 3:994–98.

37. On book export restrictions, see Kornicki, Languages, Scripts, and Chinese Texts, 130–42.

38. Edward Schafer, The Vermilion Bird: T'ang Images of the South (Berkeley: University of California Press, 1985); Hugh R. Clark, The Sinitic Encounter in Southeast China through the First Millennium CE (Honolulu: University of Hawai'i Press, 2016).

39. Yu Siu-hua, "Zhongguo yinyue de bianyuan," 62. India falls into this category because most traffic with that country passed through Central Asia. For transcribed scores of court music that reached Japan in Tang times and later, with titles that indicate many ethnic origins, see Laurence Picken, ed., Music from the Tang Court, 6 fascicles (Cambridge: Cambridge University Press, 1981–2000).

40. Cai Yan, "Hu jia shiba pai," in Yuefu shiji, comp. Guo Maoqian, 59: 860–65, followed by several later variations; for poems on the theme of Wang Zhaojun, see Yuefu shiji, 29: 424–34. Cai Yan's authorship has been questioned, as the "Hu jia" poems first appear in Guo's eleventh-century anthology. On her authorial and legendary status, see Knechtges and Chang, Ancient and Early Medieval Chinese Literature, 1:52–60. On Wang Zhaojun as national symbol, see Eugene Eoyang, "The Wang Chao-chün Legend: Configurations of the Classic," Chinese Literature: Essays, Articles, Reviews (CLEAR) 4 (1982): 3–22; Peter Perdue, "Erasing the Empire, Re-racing the Nation: Racialism and Culturalism in Imperial China," in Imperial Formations, ed. Ann Laura Stoler, Carole McGranahan, and Peter C. Perdue (Santa Fe, NM: SAR Press, 2007), 141–69; Beata Grant and Wilt Idema, The Red Brush: Writing Women of Imperial China (Cambridge, MA: Harvard University Asia Center, 2004), 91–94.

41. Chin, Savage Exchange, 214.

42. Yuefu shiji, 25:370.

43. This famous phrase, from Karl Marx, The 18th Brumaire of Louis-Napoleon, part 7 (the "sack of potatoes" argument about French peasants seeing themselves unified in a dictator), was previously used by Edward Said as an epigraph to Orientalism (New York: Pantheon, 1978). By re-citing it here, I want to point back to the different senses of "representation" in Marx's and Said's sharply different discourses.

44. Or, as indicated earlier, the act of someone masquerading as Cai Yan.

45. Timothy Wai Keung Chan, "Beyond Border and Boudoir: The Frontier in the Poetry of the Four Elites of Early Tang," in Reading Medieval Chinese Poetry, ed. Paul W. Kroll, 130–68 (Leiden: Brill, 2015). On poetic forms imitative of Central Asian music, see Elling Eide, "On Li Po," in Perspectives on the T'ang, ed. Arthur E.

Wright and Denis Twitchett (New Haven, CT: Yale University Press, 1973), 399–402. See also Kang-i Sun Chang and Stephen Owen, eds., *The Cambridge History of Chinese Literature*, 2 vols. (Cambridge: Cambridge University Press, 2013), 1: 266–67, on "northern songs" and frontier poetry.

46. Georg Wilhelm Friedrich Hegel, *Vorlesungen über die Ästhetik*, in *Werke*, 20 vols. (Frankfurt am Main: Suhrkamp, 1970), 15: 396; Hu Shi 胡適, *Baihua wenxue shi* 白話文學史 [History of Chinese vernacular literature], 1929; reprint, Taipei: Letian, 1970), 86; Zhu Guangqian 朱光潛, "Changpianshi zai Zhongguo heyi bufada" 長篇詩在中國何以不發達 [Why long narrative poetry did not develop in China, 1934]; reprinted in *Zhongguo bijiao wenxue yanjiu ziliao* 中國比較文學研究資料, ed. Beijing daxue bijiao wenxue yanjiu suo 北京大學比較文學研究所 (Beijing: Peking University Press, 1989), 220–25. For the contrary argument, see Su Meiwen 蘇美文, "Cong 'shishi' dao 'xushishi': kan Zhongguo xushishi de qiyuanshuo" 從「史詩」到「敘事詩」：看中國敘事詩的起源說 [From "epic poetry" to "narrative verse": On theories of the origin of Chinese narrative verse], *Journal of China Institute of Technology* 32 (2005): 177–93. See also Lucas Klein, *The Organization of Distance: Poetry, Translation, Chineseness* (Leiden: Brill, 2018), 72–74. It did not occur to Hegel that the *Romance of the Three Kingdoms* or the *Water-Margin Story* might be considered epics in prose.

47. Robin Kornman, Sangye Khandro, and Lama Chönam, eds. and trans., *The Epic of Gesar of Ling* (Boston: Shambhala, 2012), xv.

48. Solomon George FitzHerbert, "On the Tibetan Ge-sar Epic in the Late 18th Century: Sum-pa mkhan-po's Letters to the 6th Paṇṇ-chen Lama," *Études mongoles et sibériennes, centrasiatiques et tibétaines* 46 (2015): 1–21, https://journals.openedition.org/emscat/2602.

49. Rolf Stein, *Recherches sur l'épopée et le barde au Tibet* (Bibliothèque de l'Institut des Hautes Études chinoises, 13; Paris: Presses universitaires de France, 1959), 575.

50. Stein, *Recherches sur l'épopée*, 575–76. For a sample of the kind of literary history that is needed to trace all these centerless relations, see Daniel Selden, "Text Networks," *Ancient Narrative* 8 (2009): 1–23.

51. Stein, *Recherches sur l'épopée*, 137.

52. On this intentional conflation, fostered by the Qing, see Solomon George FitzHerbert, "The Geluk Gesar: Guandi, the Chinese God of War, in Tibetan Buddhism from the 18th to 20th Centuries," *Revue d'Études Tibétaines* 53 (2020): 178–266.

53. Jabin T. Jacob, "China in Central Asia: Controlling the Narrative," *Indian Defence Review* (January–March 2017), http://www.indiandefencereview.com/news/china-in-central-asia-controlling-the-narrative.

54. Joseph Stalin, *Marxism and the National Question* (1913), reprinted as *Marxism and the National and Colonial Question* (Leningrad: Cooperative Publishing House, 1935). On the process of designation of the "fifty-six ethnic minorities" in the 1950s, see Thomas S. Mullaney, *Coming to Terms with the Nation: Ethnic Classification in Modern China* (Berkeley: University of California Press, 2011).

55. Xi Jinping 習近平, "Zai di shisanju quanguo renmindaibiao dahui diyici huiyi shang de jianghua" 在第十三屆全國人民代表大會第一次會議上的講話 [Speech at the first meeting of the Thirteenth National Congress of the People's Representatives], March 20, 2018, http://www.gov.cn/xinwen/2018-03/20/content_5276002.htm. See also Victor Mair, "Latin Caesar→Tibetan Gesar→Xi Jinpingian Sager," https://languagelog.ldc.upenn.edu/nll/?p=37285.

Chapter 4: The Formation of China

1. See, for example, Pamela Kyle Crossley, "Thinking about Ethnicity in Early Modern China," *Late Imperial China* 11 (1990): 1–35; Frank Dikötter, *The Discourse of Race in Modern China* (Stanford, CA: Stanford University Press, 1992); Susan Blum, *Portraits of Primitives: Ordering Human Kinds in the Chinese Nation* (Lanham, MD: Rowman and Littlefield, 2001); Yuri Pines, "Beasts or Humans: Pre-Imperial Origins of the 'Sino-Barbarian' Dichotomy," in *Mongols, Turks, and Others: Eurasian Nomads and the Sedentary World*, ed. Reuven Amitai and Michal Biran (Leiden: Brill, 2004), 59–102; Wolfgang Behr, "Role of Language in Early Chinese Constructions of Ethnic Identity," *Journal of Chinese Philosophy* 37 (2010): 567–87; Thomas S. Mullaney, *Coming to Terms with the Nation: Ethnic Classification in Modern China* (Berkeley: University of California Press, 2010); Thomas S. Mullaney et al., eds., *Critical Han Studies: The History, Representation, and Identity of China's Majority* (Berkeley: University of California Press, 2012); Yang, *The Way of the Barbarians*. A rare discussion of border people who successfully entered the Chinese cultural mainstream is Siao-chen Hu, "Cultural Self-Definition of Southwest Chieftains during the Ming-Qing Transition," *Journal of Chinese Literature and Culture* 7, no. 1 (2020): 167–91.

2. Luo Zhitian, "Yi-Xia zhi bian de kaifang yu fengbi" 夷夏之辨的開放與封閉 [Opening and closure in the Yi-Han distinction], *Zhongguo wenhua* 14 (1996): 213–24, as cited and translated in Shao-yun Yang, "Reinventing the Barbarians: Rhetorical and Philosophical Uses of the *Yi-Di* in Mid-Imperial China, 600–1300" (PhD diss., University of California, Berkeley, 2014), 373. Yang's *The Way of the Barbarians* is a revised and shortened version of this dissertation. On ethnic self-definition as a reciprocal matter, see François Hartog, *Le miroir d'Hérodote: Essai sur la représentation de l'autre*, 2nd ed. (Paris: Gallimard, 2001). On language as national totem in the ancient Mediterranean, see Jonathan M. Hall, "The Role of Language in Greek Ethnicities," *Proceedings of the Cambridge Philological Society* 41 (1995): 83–100, and *Ethnic Identity in Greek Antiquity* (Cambridge: Cambridge University Press, 2000).

3. See chapter 2.

4. Chi Li [Li Ji], *The Formation of the Chinese People: An Anthropological Inquiry* (Cambridge, MA: Harvard University Press, 1928), 282, 7. On Li and debates on Chinese origins at the time, see Ge Zhaoguang, *He wei Zhongguo? Jiangyu, minzu, wenhua yu lishi* 何為中國：疆域、民族、文化與歷史 (Hong Kong: Oxford University

Press, 2014), 90–100; *What Is China? Territory, Ethnicity, Culture, and History*, trans. Michael Gibbs Hill (Cambridge, MA: Belknap Press of Harvard University Press, 2018), 76–86.

5. Ge Zhaoguang, *He wei Zhongguo?*; *What Is China?*; *Zhai zi Zhong guo: chong jian you guan "Zhongguo" de lishi lunshu* 宅茲中國：重建有關"中國"的歷史論述 (Beijing: Zhonghua, 2011), translated by Jesse Field and Qin Fang as *Here in 'China' I Dwell— Reconstructing Historical Discourses of China for Our Time* (Leiden: Brill, 2017).

6. Ernest Renan, *Qu'est-ce qu'une nation?* (Paris: Calmann-Lévy, 1882), 23.

7. Renan, *Qu'est-ce qu'une nation?*, 7, 9 (in fairly free translation).

8. Pierre Nora, ed., *Les Lieux de mémoire*, 3 vols. (Paris: Gallimard, 1984–1992).

9. Ge Zhaoguang, *Zhai zi Zhongguo*, 28. The first internal citation about cart tracks, written characters, and morals comes from the policy recommendation of Li Si to the First Emperor, as recorded in Sima Qian, *Shi ji* (*Records of the Grand Historian*), chap. 6, and the *Zhongyong*. The second refers to Eric Hobsbawm, *Nations and Nationalism since 1780: Programme, Myth, Reality* (Cambridge: Cambridge University Press, 1990), 5.

10. Ge Zhaoguang, *Zhai zi Zhongguo*, 28, as quoted and translated by Zhang Longxi in "Reconceptualizing China in Our Time: From a Chinese Perspective," *European Review* 23 (2015): 200. I have made some changes and restored some missing words.

11. Inscription from the He *zun* vessel 何尊, now kept in the Bronze Artifacts Museum of Baoji, China, as transcribed in Ma Chengyuan 馬承源, *Zhongguo qingtong qi yanjiu* 中國青銅器研究 [A study of Chinese bronzes] (Shanghai: Guji, 2002), 221, and as translated by Sarah Allan, *Buried Ideas: Legends of Abdication and Ideal Government in Early Chinese Bamboo-Slip Manuscripts* (Albany: State University of New York Press, 2015), 297. I have supplied the final phrase of the translation from Ma's transcript. For the original publication of the artifact, see Tang Lan 唐蘭, "He zun mingwen jieshi" 何尊銘文解釋 [Explanation of the He Zun inscription], *Wenwu* 1976, no. 1: 60–63.

12. See Xu Shen, *Shuowen jiezi* 說文解字 [Explanation of graphs and analysis of characters], ed. and annot. Duan Yucai 段玉裁 (reprint, Taipei: Lianjing, 1980), 12b/39a: 或，邦也。从口，戈以守其一。一，地也. Xu motivates every part of the character thus: "*Huo* means a state. It derives from 口, a boundary, and a halberd 戈 that is used to safeguard the 'one thing' 一. The 'one thing' is earth." Duan Yucai observes that "in ancient times only the 或 character existed," not the now-familiar 國. Duan's commentary adds a semiotic fable that Hobbes and Locke would have appreciated: "The reason [for the existence of the character 國] is that everybody has something to protect. And 'everybody' is the meaning of 或. As the feudal organization of society [into states and fiefdoms] spread, it began to appear that the use of 或 to designate the thing that every person protected was no longer sufficient. So then a second 口 [outer boundary] was added to make up 國. If the 'heart' radical is added, the result is 惑 ['uncertainty']. Then it became important to differentiate 'everybody' 或 from 'uncertainty' 惑, by a gradual process of increase."

13. Ge Zhaoguang, *Here in 'China' I Dwell*, 21.

14. Wang Lixiong and Kahar Barat, "Wang Lixiong fang Weiwuer xuezhe Kahaer Balati, tan Xinjiang lishi" 王力雄访维吾尔学者卡哈尔·巴拉提，谈新疆历史, blogpost dated August 7, 2013, http://bianjiang.blogspot.com/2013/08/blog-post_2551.html. English translation from "The New Dominion—Kahar Barat on Xinjiang History, Part 2: The History of the Han in Xinjiang" (expired internet resource, accessed September 24, 2018).

15. Barat speaks as a minority subject. For a standard expression of the majority opinion, see Xu Jieshun, "Understanding the Snowball Theory of the Han Nationality," in Mullaney et al., *Critical Han Studies*, 113–27: "The Chinese writing system and cultural identity constitute the most striking expression of Han cohesion. The Chinese writing system has played a unique and important role in shaping Han unity. . . . It is precisely because Chinese characters exhibit stability, clarity, and square form that there is a strong sense of identity in the psychology of the Han, serving as a cohesive force. . . . Without Chinese characters there would be no Han nationality, as they serve as a symbol of the soul and root of this group" (120–21).

16. See Claude Hagège, *Halte à la mort des langues* (Paris: Odile Jacob, 2000); Nicholas Evans, *Dying Words: Endangered Languages and What They Have to Tell Us* (Chichester, UK: Wiley-Blackwell, 2010); Neus Isern and Joaquim Fort, "Language Extinction and Linguistic Fronts," *Journal of the Royal Society Interface*, May 6, 2014, http://doi.org/10.1098/rsif.2014.0028.

17. For discussion and documentation of current conditions in Xinjiang regarding civil and cultural rights, see the Uyghur Human Rights Project website, https://uhrp.org.

18. Cf. Eric R. Wolf, *Europe and the People without History* (Berkeley: University of California Press, 1983).

19. Ian Hacking, "Making Up People," in *Historical Ontology* (Cambridge, MA: Harvard University Press, 2002), 99–120; "The Looping Effects of Human Kinds," in *Causal Cognition: A Multidisciplinary Debate*, ed. Dan Sperber, David Premack, and Ann James Premack, 351–94 (Oxford: Clarendon Press, 1995).

20. Zhang Binglin, "Zheng chou Man lun" 正仇滿論 [A rectification of anti-Manchu discourses, 1901], cited in Julia C. Schneider, *Nation and Ethnicity: Chinese Discourses on History, Historiography, and Nationalism (1900s–1920s)* (Leiden: Brill, 2017); translation slightly altered. For a study of Zhang's use of character etymology to establish historical origins for the educated class, see Lionel Jensen, *Manufacturing Confucianism: Chinese Traditions and Universal Civilization* (Durham, NC: Duke University Press, 1998), 155–58, 160–81.

21. Kornicki, *Languages, Scripts, and Chinese Texts*, 69. In South Korea today, the domain of Chinese characters has shrunk considerably (only 1,800 characters are required to be learned in high school), though *hanzi* retain their functions in such domains as classical learning, Korean literature, philosophy, Buddhism, pharmacopoeia,

and—significantly—personal names. (Each of these domains, I note, prizes both the preservation of tradition and the making of fine distinctions.)

22. On such processes that straddle the nature-culture distinction, see William Durham, *Coevolution* (Stanford, CA: Stanford University Press, 1990). Such features of culture as marriage systems, lineages, and residence patterns inevitably have an effect on the physical makeup of individuals after a few generations; group identity is never a matter of *either* nature *or* culture, except on the plane of ideological justification. Therefore I am skeptical of judgments that try to peg Chineseness as a form of cultural belonging *rather than* ethnic descent. It is both or neither.

23. Shao-yun Yang sees the *guwen* movement and the rise of *daoxue* as two forms of this call to restoration, "ethnicized orthodoxy" in the one case, "ethnocentric moralism" in the other: *The Way of the Barbarians*, 15, 21.

24. Qiu Jun, *Daxue yanyi bu* (SKQS ed.), chap. 82, "Guang jiaohua yi biansu" 廣教化以變俗, 9a (abbreviating Ma Duanlin 馬端臨, *Wenxian tongkao* 文獻通考 46.430–31).

25. Phillips observes that "visions of political community were needed that could not only motivate and justify continued conquest, but also bind local collaborators to imperial structures and stabilise the hierarchical international orders that developed around emerging empires" ("Civilising Missions and the Rise of International Hierarchies," 705). Curiously, recent publications on the intra-Asian version of the "civilizing mission" topos focus only on the Qing. For another example, see Vickers, "A Civilising Mission with Chinese Characteristics?"

26. Qiu Jun, *Daxue yanyi bu*, chap. 82, 10b.

27. Qiu Jun, *Daxue yanyi bu*, chap. 82, 15b–16a (condensing a passage from Wei Shou, *Wei shu*, 32:761).

28. Qiu Jun, *Daxue yanyi bu*, chap. 82, 9a–b.

29. Hayden White, *Metahistory: The Historical Imagination in Nineteenth-Century Europe* (Baltimore, MD: Johns Hopkins University Press, 1973), 9–10, 54, 79, 190.

30. Li Zehou, *The Chinese Aesthetic Tradition*, trans. Majia Bell Samei (Honolulu: University of Hawai'i Press, 2010), 90, 219, 100. Original publication: *Huaxia meixue* (Hong Kong: Sanlian, 1988).

31. Luo Yuming, *A Concise History of Chinese Literature*, trans. Ye Yang, 2 vols. (Leiden: Brill, 2011), 1: 2, 4–5, 33.

32. Alexander Beecroft, *Authorship and Cultural Identity in Early Greece and China: Patterns of Literary Circulation* (Cambridge: Cambridge University Press, 2010); *An Ecology of World Literature: From Antiquity to the Present Day* (London: Verso, 2015).

33. Cf. John D. Barrow and Frank J. Tipler, *The Anthropic Cosmological Principle* (Oxford: Oxford University Press, 1988). See also Hugh R. Clark, "What's the Matter with 'China'? A Critique of Teleological History," *Journal of Asian Studies* 77 (2018): 295–314; Andrew Chittick, "Thinking Regionally in Early Medieval Studies: A Manifesto," *Early Medieval China* 26 (2020): 3–18.

34. Du Fu, "You gan wu shou" 有感五首, 2, in Qiu Zhao'ao 仇兆鰲, *Du shi xiangzhu* 杜詩詳註, 5 vols. (Beijing: Zhonghua shuju, 1979), 2:971; translation slightly modified from Stephen Owen, trans., *The Poetry of Du Fu*, 4 vols. (Berlin: de Gruyter, 2017), 3:193.

35. For the epithets, see *Du shi xiangzhu*, 3:1044, 1050, 1161. This is hardly an exhaustive list.

36. See chapter 2, note 37.

37. Bdos-nams-rgyal-mtshan, *The Mirror Illuminating the Royal Genealogies*, trans. Per K. Sørensen, in Sørensen, *Tibetan Royal Historiography: The Mirror Illuminating the Royal Genealogies, an Annotated Translation of the XIVth Century Tibetan Chronicle rGyal-rabs gsal-ba'i me-long* (Wiesbaden: Harrassowitz, 1994), 417–21. I have edited slightly for style. Note that the Jincheng Princess brought with her manuals of trades and crafts that, presumably, were not considered to touch on matters of state.

38. Brandon Dotson, "The Old Tibetan Annals (Version II)," in *The Old Tibetan Annals: An Annotated Translation of Tibet's First History*, trans. Dotson (Vienna: Österreichische Akademie der Wissenschaften, 2009), 132.

39. Quoting Shao Yong via Li Zhi 李贄: see "Da Geng Zhongcheng lun dan" 答耿中丞論淡, in Li Zhi, *Fen shu* 焚書 (Beijing: Zhonghua shuju, 1975), 24; translation in Rivi Handler-Spitz, Pauline C. Lee, and Haun Saussy, eds. and trans., *A Book to Burn and a Book to Keep (Hidden): Selected Writings of Li Zhi* (New York: Columbia University Press, 2016), 46.

40. James Joyce, *Ulysses* (New York: Vintage, 1986), 28.

Chapter 5: Exiles and Emissaries amid Their New Neighbors

1. *Li ji*, "Da xue," sec. 14, in *Shisan jing zhushu*, 5:3634.

2. For versions of this story, see Li Fang 李昉 et al., comp., *Taiping guangji* 太平廣記, chap. 153, 10 vols. (Beijing: Zhonghua shuju, 1961), 3:1100; and Madeline K. Spring, "T'ang Landscapes of Exile," *Journal of the American Oriental Society* 117, no. 2 (1997): 312–23. On exile and travel in imperial China, see Li Xingsheng 李興盛, *Zhongguo liuren shi* 中國流人史 [A history of exile in China] (Harbin: Heilongjiang renmin chubanshe, 2013); Richard E. Strassberg, *Inscribed Landscapes: Travel Writing from Imperial China* (Berkeley: University of California Press, 1994); Joanna Waley-Cohen, *Exile in Mid-Qing China: Banishment to Xinjiang, 1758–1820* (New Haven, CT: Yale University Press, 1991); Carolyn Cartier, *Globalizing South China* (Chichester, UK: Wiley, 2011); Ping Wang and Nicholas Morrow Williams, eds., *Southern Identity and Southern Estrangement in Medieval Chinese Poetry* (Hong Kong: Hong Kong University Press, 2015).

3. Schafer, *The Vermilion Bird*, 135.

4. Han Yu, "Song Qu Ce xu," 送區冊序 [Instructions for Qu Ce], in *Han Changli wenji jiaozhu* 韓昌黎文集校注, 155–56.

5. Cf. Han Yu, "Ji eyu wen" 祭鱷魚文 [Offering to the crocodiles], in *Han Changli wenji jiaozhu*, 329–31.

6. Liu Zongyuan, "Liuzhou dongmeng" 柳州峒氓, in *Liu Zongyuan shi jianshi* 柳宗元詩箋釋, ed. Wang Guo'an 王國安 (Shanghai: Guji, 1993), 330. The final line alludes to *Zhuangzi*, chap. 1: "A man of Song went to Yue to sell ceremonial caps, but as the Yue cropped their hair and tattooed their bodies, they had no use for such things" 宋人資章甫而適諸越，越人斷髮文身，無所用之. Guo Qingfan 郭慶藩, ed., *Zhuangzi jishi* 莊子集釋 (Beijing: Zhonghua shuju, 1962), 31.

7. "Min sheng fu" 閔生賦, in *Liu Zongyuan ji* 柳宗元集 (Beijing: Zhonghua shuju, 1979), 59.

8. "Zhao hai gu wen" 招海賈文, in *Liu Zongyuan ji*, 508.

9. *Liu Zongyuan ji*, 734–59; translated as "Eight Pieces from Yongzhou Prefecture" in Richard E. Strassberg, ed. and trans., *Inscribed Landscapes: Travel Writing from Imperial China* (Berkeley: University of California Press, 1994), 141–47.

10. *Liu Zongyuan ji*, 455–56.

11. *Liu Zongyuan ji*, 535–36.

12. On Liu's and other exiles' letters, see Anna M. Shields, "The Inscription of Emotion in Mid-Tang Collegial Letters," in *A History of Chinese Letters and Epistolary Culture*, ed. Antje Richter (Leiden: Brill, 2015), 675–720.

13. See, for example, "Yu Li Hanlin Jian shu" 與李翰林建書 [Letter to Hanlin academician Li Jian], *Liu Zongyuan ji*, 800–803.

14. See Edward Schafer, *Shore of Pearls: Hainan Island in Early Times* (Berkeley: University of California Press, 1970), 85–101; Kathleen Tomlonovic, "Poetry of Exile and Return: A Study of Su Shi (1037–1101)," PhD diss., University of Washington, 1989; James Hargett, "Clearing the Apertures and Getting in Tune: The Hainan Exile of Su Shi (1037–1101)," *Journal of Song-Yuan Studies* 30 (2000): 141–67; Ronald Egan, *Word, Image and Deed in the Life of Su Shi* (Cambridge, MA: Harvard East Asia Center, 1994), 207–60; Yang Zhiyi, "Return to an Inner Utopia: Su Shi's Transformation of Tao Qian in his Exile Poetry," *T'oung Pao* 99 (2013): 329–78.

15. *Su Shi shiji* 蘇軾詩集, 7:2322, 2324.

16. *Su Shi shiji*, 7:2322–23. The grouping is certainly not Su Shi's, as the poems were assembled from anecdote collections.

17. *Taiping yulan* 368.2.13.

18. Fan Huijun 范會俊 and Zhu Yihui 朱逸輝, eds., *Su Shi Hainan shiwen xuanzhu* 蘇軾海南詩文選注, 99, as quoted in Hargett, "Su Shi's Hainan Exile," 156 (translation altered). The poem does not appear in Su Shi's collections and may not be authentic. "Dongpo" (Eastern Slope) was an informal sobriquet Su adopted late in life.

19. *Su Shi shiji*, 7:2266. For another translation, see the discussion in Yang Zhiyi, "Return to an Inner Utopia," 346–47.

20. *Su Shi shiji*, 7:2281. See also Hargett, "Opening the Apertures," 154: Su's friendship with the locals can be seen as both a survival strategy and "a sort of protest or complaint against those who had exiled him."

21. Yang, "Return to an Inner Utopia," 347.

22. Su Shi, "He Tao 'Quan nong' liu shou" 和陶勸農六首, *Su Shi shiji*, 7:2254–57.

23. Su Shi, "Shu Liu Zihou 'Niu fu' hou" 書柳子厚牛賦後, *Su Shi wenji*, 5:2058.

24. Qiu Jun's *Daxue yanyi bu* is, as its title indicates, an elaborate augmentation cum commentary on the classical text *Da xue*, "The Great Learning," long adopted as a kind of propaedeutic to Confucian values: as an imaginary address to the throne, it appends discursive appendixes and historical examples to each word of the original text.

25. See Hacking, "The Looping Effects of Human Kinds."

26. Crossley, "Thinking about Ethnicity in Early Modern China," 2.

27. The suspicious understanding of Su's Hainan writings sketched here echoes Claude Lévi-Strauss's misgivings about intercultural communication as expressed in *Tristes Tropiques* (Paris: Plon, 1955), 448. For a polemic against the effects of the first agricultural revolution, see James C. Scott, *Against the Grain: A Deep History of the Earliest States* (New Haven, CT: Yale University Press, 2017).

28. On this and other ethnographies bridging Chinese and Mongol worlds, see Ming Tak Ted Hui, "Journeys to the West: Travelogues and Discursive Power in the Making of the Mongol Empire," *Journal of Chinese Literature and Culture* 7, no. 1 (2020): 60–86. For a topographic study of the places named in Li Zhichang's work, see Chen Zhengxiang 陳正祥, *Changchun Zhenren Xiyouji de dilixue pingzhu* 長春真人西遊記的地理學評註 (Hong Kong: Geographical Research Centre, Chinese University of Hong Kong, 1968).

29. Li Zhichang, *Changchun zhenren Xiyouji* 長春真人西遊記 (Shanghai: Zhonghua shuju, 1936), 18–19. Cf. Arthur Waley, trans., *Travels of an Alchemist* (London: Routledge, 1931), 67–68. Waley omits the poems from his abridged translation.

30. Nicola Di Cosmo, *Ancient China and Its Enemies: The Rise of Nomadic Power in East Asian History* (Cambridge: Cambridge University Press, 2002), 10.

31. Di Cosmo, *Ancient China and Its Enemies*, 271.

32. Sima Qian, *Shiji* (Beijing: Zhonghua shuju, 1959), 10:3289.

33. James A. Millward, *Beyond the Pass: Economy, Ethnicity and Empire in Qing Central Asia, 1759–1864* (Stanford, CA: Stanford University Press, 1998), 27–30; Peter C. Perdue, *China Marches West: The Qing Conquest of Central Eurasia* (Cambridge, MA: Harvard University Press, 2005), 254–91.

34. "When I went with the troops to the Western Regions, I often had to write official communiqués at short notice, so there was no opportunity to write poetry. If a line or couplet came to mind, I forgot it as soon as the mood passed. The 160 poems of *Wulumuqi zashi* were composed on the basis of memory after I returned home; they were not written contemporaneously with the events they describe" 余從軍西域時，草奏草檄，日不暇給，遂不復吟詠。或得一聯一句，亦境過輒忘。《烏魯木齊雜詩》百六十首，皆歸途追憶而成，非當日作也。Ji Yun, *Yuewei caotang biji* 閱微草堂筆記 [Notes from the grass hut of minute observation] (Taipei: Da Zhongguo tushu gongsi, 2002), 315. For a roughly contemporary and somewhat similar series of eighty-two quatrains describing life among the alien peoples of the Southwest, see

David M. Deal and Laura Hostetler, trans., *The Art of Ethnography: A Chinese "Miao Album"* (Seattle: University of Washington Press, 2006).

35. Qian Daxin 錢大昕, *Qianyantang wenji* 潛研堂文集 (SBCK ed.), 26. 1a. On the collection, see also L. J. Newby, "The Chinese Literary Conquest of Xinjiang," *Modern China* 25, no. 4 (1999): 451–74; Millward, *Beyond the Pass*, 134–35, 283; Waley-Cohen, *Exile in Mid-Qing China*, 4–6, 8, 141, 148, 150–56, 159; and Wang Pengkai 王鵬凱, "Cengjing Xiyu wanli xing—Ji Yun de Xinjiang shuxie" 曾經西域萬里行—紀昀的新疆書寫 [I once traversed ten thousand miles of Western terrain—Ji Yun's Xinjiang writing], *Donghai daxue tushuguan guanxun* 157 (2014): 43–65.

36. Ji Yun, *Wulumuqi zashi* 烏魯木齊雜詩 (*Congshu jicheng* edition), 1.

37. The "Southern Branch" alludes to "Nanke taishou zhuan" 南柯太守傳 (*Taiping guangji*, chap. 475), a story about a man who dreamed about attaining office and riches in the Kingdom of the Ants, only to discover on waking that it was all an illusion.

38. On the Torghuts' advance to the Volga in the early seventeenth century, see Michael Khodarkovsky, *Where Two Worlds Met: The Russian State and the Kalmyk Nomads, 1600–1771* (Ithaca, NY: Cornell University Press, 1992), 74–80.

39. *Mencius* 1 A 6, here in Legge's translation (*The Chinese Classics*, 2:137). Parallel passages, with 猶 for 由: *Mencius* 4 A 9, 6 A 6.

40. Ji Yun, "Yu shi Tuerhute quanbu guishun shi" 御試土爾扈特全部歸順詩 [On the return to obedience of the entire Torghut nation: By imperial commission], in *Ji Wenda gong yiji* 紀文達公遺集 [Collected writings of the late Ji Yun, 1812] (reprint, Shanghai: Guji, 2010), juan 7, 17b–19a. On this event, see James Millward, "What Did the Qianlong Court Mean by *Huairou Yuanren*?" in *How Mongolia Matters: War, Law, and Society*, ed. Morris Rossabi (Leiden: Brill, 2017), 19–34. Qian Daxin, Ji Yun's friend and prefacer, had written a similar poem after Qing victory over the Zungars in 1759: see Ori Sela, *China's Philological Turn: Scholars, Textualism, and the Dao in the Eighteenth Century* (New York: Columbia University Press, 2018), 46.

41. *Huainanzi*, chap. 15, in Liu Wendian 劉文典, ed., *Huainan honglie jijie* 淮南鴻烈集解, 2 vols. (Beijing: Zhonghua shuju, 1989), 2:499; the passage is quoting the First Emperor's propaganda steles ironically, since the argument concerns the Second Emperor's inability to keep his power intact.

42. Guo Qingfan, *Zhuangzi jishi*, 190.

Conclusion

1. See Millward, *Beyond the Pass*; Hodong Kim, *Holy War in China: The Muslim Rebellion and State in Chinese Central Asia, 1864–1877* (Stanford, CA: Stanford University Press, 2004); L. J. Newby, *The Empire and the Khanate: A Political History of Qing Relations with Khoqand, c. 1760–1860* (Leiden: Brill, 2005).

2. Cf. Ge, *What Is China?*, 122–23; *He wei Zhongguo?*, 145–46.

3. Willard Van Orman Quine, *From a Logical Point of View* (Cambridge, MA: Harvard University Press, 1953), 1.

4. Benedict de Spinoza, "Letter 50" to Jarig Jelles (1674), in *Works of Spinoza*, trans. R. H. M. Elwes (1883; reprint, New York: Dover, 1955), 2:369–70: "As to the doctrine that figure is negation and not anything positive, it is plain that the whole of matter considered indefinitely can have no figure, and that figure can only exist in finite and determinate bodies. . . . This determination . . . does not appertain to the thing according to its being, but on the contrary, is its non-being. As then figure is nothing else than determination, and determination is negation, figure, as has been said, can be nothing but negation." Spinoza's reasoning about geometrical figures would apply as well to other bounded objects such as nations and concepts. Ferdinand de Saussure says similarly of signs that "in language, there are only differences without positive terms": *Course in General Linguistics* (1916), trans. Wade Baskin, ed. Perry Meisel and Haun Saussy (New York: Columbia University Press, 2011), 120.

5. I insist on the plural. The use of "civilization" (to praise) and "empire" (to blame) is too often made, by omission, singular. The tacit object-choices of those who set themselves against particular forms of domination confirm this singularity in an unfortunate way. If seventy-five years of postcolonial theory have taught us nothing more than the necessity of condemning *European* empires, that is a disappointingly narrow and Eurocentric conclusion to draw. Such an education does not prepare us to understand even Europe, let alone the rest of the world as it has been and is becoming. Showing what Sinocentrism has in common with Eurocentrisms and other pernicious -centrisms, as I have tried to do here, might contribute to a remedy. For a discussion aimed at generating "meeting points between Western and Chinese colonial discourses," see Emma Jinhua Teng, *Taiwan's Imagined Geography: Chinese Colonial Travel Writing and Pictures, 1683–1895* (Cambridge, MA: Harvard University Asia Center, 2004), 249–58.

6. On avoidance as a cultural marker, see Georges Devereux and Edwin M. Loeb, "Antagonistic Acculturation," *American Sociological Review* 8 (1943): 133–47.

7. See, for example, "Text Networks"; Daniel L. Selden, "Mapping the Alexander Romance," in *The Alexander Romance in Persia and the East*, ed. Richard Stoneman, Kyle Erickson, and Ian Netton (Groningen, the Netherlands: Barkhuis, 2012), 19–59.

8. On the extension of the model of the isogloss, taken from dialect studies, to cultural forms (and, in a speculative leap, to political geography) by the early Slavic structuralists, see Patrick Sériot, *Structure et totalité: Les origines intellectuelles du structuralisme en Europe centrale et orientale* (Paris: Presses universitaires de France, 1999).

9. Victor Fleming, dir., *The Wizard of Oz* (1939; Burbank, CA: Warner Home Video, 2009); Laurence Sterne, *A Sentimental Journey through France and Italy* (Oxford: Humphrey Milford, 1928), 1.

10. Ludwig Wittgenstein, *Tractatus Logico-Philosophicus*, trans. C. K. Ogden (London: Routledge & Kegan Paul, 1981), 149. Imagine the case of someone who says, "Limits? My language has no limits."

11. On the cliché of the two "schools," see César Dominguez, Haun Saussy, and Darío Villanueva, *Introducing Comparative Literature: New Trends and Applications* (New York: Routledge, 2015), 23.

12. See Haun Saussy, "The Comparative History of East Asian Literatures: A Sort of Manifesto," *Modern Languages Open* 1 (2018): 20, https://www.modernlanguagesopen .org/articles/10.3828/mlo.v0i0.206/.

13. A project of the International Comparative Literature Association, under way since 2015, seeks to recount this history in a series of forthcoming volumes. See Haun Saussy, "ICLA Research Committee: A Comparative History of East Asian Litera-tures," *Recherche Littéraire / Literary Research* 33 (2017): 304–6, http://www.ailc-icla .org/wp-content/uploads/2018/07/Recherche-littéraire-2017-vol-33.pdf.

14. Istvan Banyai, *Zoom* (New York: Random House, 1995).

TRANSLATION / TRANSNATION

Series Editor Emily Apter

INDEX

A NOTE ON THE TYPE

This book has been composed in Arno, an Old-style serif typeface in the
classic Venetian tradition, designed by Robert Slimbach at Adobe.